**ORACLE®**   *Oracle Press*™

Oracle CRM On Demand Embedded Analytics

Michael D. Lairson

Mc Graw Hill

New York   Chicago   San Francisco
Lisbon   London   Madrid   Mexico City   Milan
New Delhi   San Juan   Seoul   Singapore   Sydney   Toronto

The *McGraw-Hill* Companies

Library of Congress Cataloging-in-Publication Data

Lairson, Michael D.
    Oracle CRM on demand embedded analytics / Michael D. Lairson.
        p. cm.
    ISBN 978-0-07-174536-9 (pbk.)
    1. Oracle (Computer file) 2. Relational databases. 3. Database searching.
4. Automatic indexing. 5. Business report writing—Data processing. I. Title.
QA76.9.D32L3526 2011
005.75'75—dc22   2010049870

McGraw-Hill books are available at special quantity discounts to use as premiums and sales promotions, or for use in corporate training programs. To contact a representative, please e-mail us at bulksales@ mcgraw-hill.com.

Oracle CRM On Demand Embedded Analytics

1 2 3 4 5 6 7 8 9 0   QFR QFR   1 0 9 8 7 6 5 4 3 2 1

ISBN   978-0-07-174536-9
MHID   0-07-174536-X

Associate Acquisitions Editor Meghan Riley	**Technical Editor** Elizabeth Osso	**Composition** Glyph International
Editorial Supervisor Patty Mon	**Copy Editor** Lisa McCoy	**Illustration** Glyph International
Project Manager Tania Andrabi, Glyph International	**Proofreader** Carol Shields	**Art Director, Cover** Jeff Weeks
Acquisitions Coordinator Stephanie Evans	**Indexer** Ted Laux	**Cover Designer** Pattie Lee
	Production Supervisor Jim Kussow	

To my loving and patient wife, Susan.

About the Author

Michael Lairson began his career in 1993 in Charlotte, North Carolina, as a technical writer after earning a BA in English at the University of North Carolina, Charlotte. Mike moved into the instructional design field in 1995 and prepared training materials that ranged from training manuals to high-end multimedia applications for many companies. During this time, Mike returned to UNC Charlotte to earn an M.Ed. in instructional systems technology. Continuing to broaden his experience and explore professional interest in evaluation and analysis led Mike to Siebel Systems, where he worked as a certification exams developer for several years. In this role he created the certification exams and the study materials for most of the Siebel Certification exams and performed a large amount of reporting of exam data.

In the process of writing the CRM On Demand exam, Mike began to take great interest in the application and moved to the training team as part of the professional services organization. He has since continued to expand his knowledge of the application and has established himself as an expert resource for Oracle CRM On Demand, and in particular the reporting tool.

Mike remained with Oracle after the Siebel merger and played a key role in the development of the Advanced Analytics Workshop training offered by Oracle, as well as many other CRM On Demand training classes.

In September 2008, Mike's first book, *Oracle CRM On Demand Reporting,* was published and immediately became the definitive source of information on developing reports with Answers On Demand. Also look for his second book, *Oracle CRM On Demand Dashboards,* to add dashboards to your business intelligence skill set. Third in the series is *Oracle CRM On Demand Combined Analyses.* Currently working for Intelenex, Mike holds the position of manager of business intelligence services and regularly develops analytic reports and dashboards for his customers and offers custom training in Oracle CRM On Demand reporting. When not working, Mike spends time with his wife and two sons, and is an active member of his church, the Knights of Columbus, and Boy Scouts of America.

About the Technical Editor

Elizabeth Osso, CMC, is a principal SaaS Consultant, Lucid Blue Consulting, Inc.

A certified management consultant, since 1995, Elizabeth has consulted with organizations on the selection, implementation, and operations of customer relationship management, human resources, and financial management solutions. During her tenure at Oracle Corporation (previously Siebel Systems), she worked with clients on the implementation of CRM On Demand, assisting them in leveraging CRM On Demand and analytics to support their business processes. She has spoken in both Canada and the United States on various topics, including customer adoption and using Analytics for CRM On Demand at Oracle Open World and various user groups. Recently, her time is focused on getting the most out of the "cloud" for her clients, including CRM and customer portals.

A graduate of Durham College, Elizabeth is currently working on an advanced degree in information technology at Athabasca University.

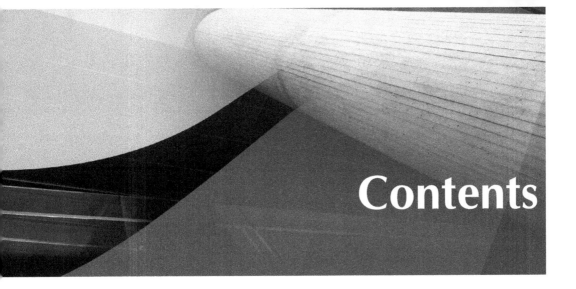

Contents

ACKNOWLEDGMENTS xi
INTRODUCTION xiii

1 Getting Started with Embedded Analytics **1**
About Oracle CRM On Demand 2
Access Control for Report Developers 3
Administrator Access Controls Required
    for Embedding Reports 5
        Company Profile Setting Affecting
            Reports and Dashboards 7
        User Profile Settings Affecting Reports 9
Introduction to Embedded Analytics 10
The Role of Embedded Analytics
    in Oracle CRM On Demand 14
The Importance of Planning 15
HTML You Should Know for Embedded Analytics 16
        Structure Tags 17
        Basic Text Tags 17
        List Tags 19
        Link Tags 20
        Image Tag 20
        Table Tags 21
        Inline Frame Tag 21

2 Designing Reports for Embedding **25**
Basic Report Development 26
    Adding, Removing, and Reordering Columns 29
    Formatting Columns 29
    Sorting Columns 36
    Filtering Report Data 36
    Report Views 40
    Pivot Tables 65
    Pivot Charts 80

3 Linking Reports **85**
URLs in Oracle CRM On Demand 86
    Go URL Tags 92
Linking Reports to Other Reports 99
    Navigate Function 99
    Include a Report Hyperlink in a Formula 102
    Include a Hyperlink in a Narrative View 104
Linking Reports to Detail and Edit Screens 105
    ActionLinks 105
    Custom Text Format Links 108
    Formula Links 113
    Hyperlink in a Narrative 114
    Links to Edit Screens 114
Web Link Fields 115
Dashboard Links 118
    Linking from a Dashboard 118
    Linking to a Dashboard 123
    Linking to a Filtered Dashboard 124
Special Links 124
    E-mail Links 124
    External Links 125
    Web Tab Links 126

4 Embedding Reports **127**
Reports on the Home Tab 129
Reports Inside Dashboards 133
    Display Results 135
    Report Links 136
    Show View 138

Modify Request 139

Rename 139

Delete 140

Using Inline Frames to Embed Reports 140

Embedding Reports Inside Reports 141

Embedding Dashboards Inside Reports 145

Embedding Reports Inside Applets 147

Embedding Reports and Dashboards on a Web Tab 149

Custom Report Menu 152

Role-Based Dashboard Access 153

Custom Search Tab 153

Report Widget 154

External Sites Embedded Inside Reports 157

Index **161**

Acknowledgments

With each book, the list of people who have supported and influenced me grows longer. I love this work because I so often learn something during the process of teaching the skills I try to describe in my books. I wish I could remember it all, and wish I could remember everyone who taught me something along the way.

I, of course, thank my wife Susan and my boys Robbie and David, who have been so patient with me and so giving of family time so I could produce this and other books. Now that I have finished this series of books, I look forward to showing you how much I love you and how much you mean to me.

Others who have shown me support, encouraged me, or challenged me along the way—I thank you. Listed in no particular order: Elizabeth Osso, who provided technical editing on this book, Jeff H., Noni, Dave and Kit K., Doug C., Erin W., Colleen J., Suzanne L., Jared W., Ray G., Greg B., Greg T., Connie S., Julie G., Kiran, Madhu, Prashant, Alexandra B., Jayd, Binh, Zephrin, Alex N., Robert D., Louis P., Leslie P., Kelly S., Steve B., and James O.

I would also like to acknowledge all of those at Oracle who work with the Oracle CRM On Demand product on a daily basis. Many of you have told me personally how much you appreciate my work, and it pleases me to know that I have helped you and your customers in some way.

Introduction

Analytics (or business intelligence) is one of the hottest topics in corporate boardrooms around the world. It seems that the ability to report on business data is a base requirement for many software purchase decisions, and is a differentiating factor in the hosted CRM or Software as a Service (SaaS) selection criteria. The ability to build powerful reports is something that is becoming more common as this trend continues. The additional ability to deliver these powerful reports to the users of the systems is a bit more elusive. Well-built, insightful analytic reports are only useful if the individuals who need that information are able to access and understand the reports without a great deal of effort.

Software as a Service is quickly becoming a norm, rather than an emerging trend. The current economy may have driven more companies to this software model whereby companies pay for licenses to access software on external servers rather than pay for an installation of the software on their own servers. This is often a more economical model as companies do not have the additional cost of software, hardware, and support personnel.

Oracle CRM On Demand is one such SaaS application, and the topic of this book. With Oracle CRM On Demand, users have access to a world-class customer relationship management application that includes an extremely robust business intelligence tool called Oracle Answers On Demand. Oracle Answers On Demand is included with each license, rather than a separate cost.

About Oracle CRM On Demand

Oracle CRM On Demand's roots begin with Sales.com. Sales.com was the first hosted CRM product for Siebel Systems. Siebel Systems was the leader in the CRM industry at the time, but the world was not yet ready for Sales.com, and that service shut down in 2001 due to a lack of interest. A mere two years later, in 2003, Siebel reemerged in the CRM Software as a Service market with Siebel CRM OnDemand. Shortly thereafter, Siebel Systems acquired UpShot, another trailblazer in the hosted CRM industry. UpShot's technology was rolled into Siebel CRM OnDemand. The next acquisition affecting the hosted CRM product was the purchase of Ineto. Ineto's technology added call center hosting to the Siebel CRM OnDemand offering.

Fast forward to early 2006 and Oracle's completed acquisition of Siebel Systems, and we see a leading hosted CRM application suddenly gain the backing of a huge software empire and the support and research and development that come with it. Rather than get lost in the rich mix of Oracle software products and a set of products and services already bearing the "OnDemand" moniker, Siebel CRM OnDemand became Oracle CRM On Demand and continued to thrive. Since that acquisition, Oracle has continued to push out additional versions of the application, with aggressive and impressive enhancements that continue to set the standard for hosted CRM applications.

Oracle CRM On Demand is a full-service suite of hosted CRM that includes core service, sales, and marketing components. Hosted call center and e-mail marketing are two additional options that integrate fully with the application. The extensive CRM functionality of Oracle CRM On Demand includes marketing campaign management, lead management, revenue forecasting, sales opportunity management, account management, contact management, service request and solution management, and quota management. Offline access and integration with e-mail applications and mobile devices are also available. Seamless integration with back-office applications is also available using prebuilt integration points (PIPs) or custom web services.

Most important to the readers of this book, Oracle CRM On Demand includes the Answers On Demand tool, which offers extensive and powerful embedded analytics functionality. Reports developed within Answers On Demand may be run from within Oracle CRM On Demand by clicking a hyperlink on the reports screen or, as I will describe in this book, can be embedded throughout the application.

About This Book

A couple of years ago, I began keeping notes of tips and tricks and things I learned as I struggled to develop reports for my customers. That effort led to my first book, *Oracle CRM On Demand Reporting* (McGraw-Hill/Professional, 2008), as I found myself overwhelmed with the features and possibilities of analytics in Oracle CRM On Demand and the functions at my disposal. I wrote that book in order to have a single resource that I could reference as I built reports. As a nice secondary benefit, I was able to assist many others with their reports in the form of that reference.

I have continued to teach reporting workshops and keep up with the enhancements within Oracle CRM On Demand and the ever-expanding demands of the users of the application. I have noticed some things about how reports and dashboards are being implemented by companies using Oracle CRM On Demand. One of the most prominent trends is in the deployment of business intelligence within the application.

It is a widely accepted belief that business intelligence, or analytics, is critical to business success. Analytics is almost always a key factor in the decision to purchase Oracle CRM On Demand licenses, and any application that does not provide or contribute to business intelligence capabilities is quickly brushed aside.

So often, people and companies who implement Oracle CRM On Demand think of configuring the application and developing and deploying reports as two separate, mutually exclusive phases of the overall CRM implementation. This is a trend that is quickly fading, and companies are recognizing the value of not only having access to analytical tools, but also integrating the business intelligence gained from a CRM application into the business processes. Putting reports in the hands of the users by embedding them into the application in the places that the user needs and benefits from the information provides a valuable benefit and return on your CRM investment.

My hope is that this book will help you take full advantage of Oracle CRM On Demand reports and dashboards by embedding your analytics throughout the application.

The book begins in Chapter 1 with a comprehensive overview of the concept of embedded analytics. As you look to link and embed reports throughout Oracle CRM On Demand, a basic understanding of some web concepts and HTML are helpful. Chapter 1 exposes you to these concepts and prepares you for the techniques described in the chapters that follow.

Since I cannot assume that everyone who picks up this book is an expert report developer and Oracle CRM On Demand administrator, I offer Chapter 2, where the most important report development skills are described. Of course, for a more in-depth study of report development, you should invest in a copy of *Oracle CRM On Demand Reporting* (McGraw-Hill/Professional, 2008).

Chapter 3 is a detailed study of making reports accessible through hyperlinks into reports, and embedding reports into the business process by including links from reports to other parts of the application. The URLs described in Chapter 3 are also critical to the processes described in the chapter that follows. Chapter 4 builds on the linking concept with embedding reports into a variety of places within Oracle CRM On Demand. Presenting reports to your users almost anywhere in the application makes business intelligence part of the actual business processes that your users are completing each day using Oracle CRM On Demand. This leads to greater efficiency, greater accuracy, and improved user adoption.

How to Use This Book

This book is more than just a detailed explanation of processes for Oracle CRM On Demand Embedded Analytics. As in my other books, which I hope you already have well-worn copies of, this book contains valuable experience from hours upon hours of struggle with the most interesting and challenging reporting requirements. As with any skill, the best way to develop is through practice, and it is my hope that you will benefit from the many hours of my own practice. It is not a replacement for your time and effort, of course, but it certainly is a nice head start.

What I have developed for you here is a detailed quick reference for a specific usage of reporting within Oracle CRM On Demand. There are a number of skills that are not specific to Oracle that you will call on within these pages, including HTML and JavaScript. These skills are not the main topic of this book, but you will find examples of where and how they are used, which are easy for you to duplicate in your Oracle CRM On Demand application.

Novice or seasoned veteran, whether you read it to learn or use it as a reference tool, I hope and believe your use of embedded analytics, and ultimately your users, will benefit from the information offered in this book.

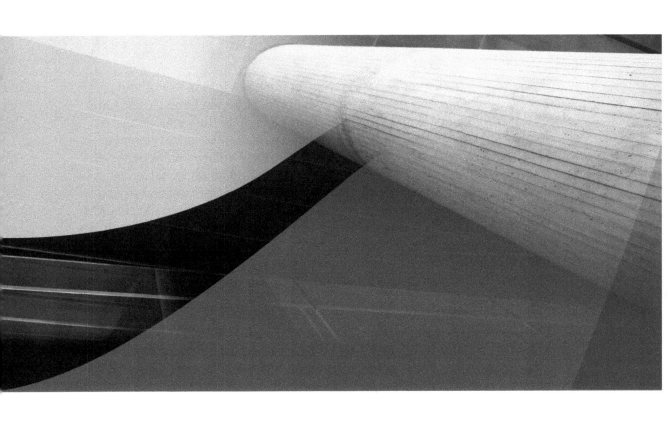

CHAPTER
1

Getting Started with
Embedded Analytics

his chapter describes some of the basic information about the report development environment within Oracle CRM On Demand and provides an introduction to the methodology of embedded analytics. If you have read, or keep for reference, a copy of my first book *Oracle CRM On Demand Reports* (McGraw-Hill/Professional, 2008), you may be familiar with Oracle On Demand Answers. If you are new to Oracle CRM On Demand and picked up this book to learn how to build, create, and embed reports in Oracle CRM On Demand, I highly recommend that you begin with the earlier book. This book will review some of the basics, but is not intended to be a complete reference. Experience with report development is important for you to successfully embed reports throughout the Oracle CRM On Demand application.

First, we will discuss some basic information about the Oracle CRM On Demand environment and the administrative settings that are necessary for access to report development tools within the application. Since we are also embedding reports throughout the application, some additional administrative access is required beyond report development.

About Oracle CRM On Demand

One of the most difficult concepts that my customers struggle with is also a most basic and core concept that is critical for the report and dashboard developer to comprehend. Oracle CRM On Demand is a hosted application. That means that the software you are accessing when you sign in to Oracle CRM On Demand is not installed on your computer. You are, in most cases, not accessing servers owned by your company. In fact, you are accessing software installed on servers in an Oracle data center, and you are most likely sharing that server space with several other companies also using Oracle CRM On Demand. This is how a multitenant software as a service (SaaS) environment works, and many companies are benefiting from the reduced hardware costs and overhead that come with this type of software service.

Your Oracle CRM On Demand license allows you to access the application through your web browser. The databases that you are viewing through the Oracle CRM On Demand user interface are typically located in a data center, and the level of access you have to the database is not that of a database administrator (DBA). Your company does not need to provide a DBA to maintain the database on the Oracle CRM On Demand server (or pod).

Within your instance of Oracle CRM On Demand, you can configure the screens; add and remove fields; change the names and appearances of screens; and build your own lists, reports, and dashboards. These are the things you do to make Oracle CRM On Demand fit your business. Some things, however, you are not able to do within your Oracle CRM On Demand instance. You cannot, for example, change the underlying schema of the database. You cannot configure the underlying data warehouse or change the ETL (Extract, Transform, Load) schedule yourself, but you may be able to negotiate such changes with Oracle depending on your licensing. Single-tenant customers (those not sharing servers with other customers) may have more flexibility in this area than multitenant customers.

Another important concept that goes along with working in this hosted environment is that you are working on the Internet. Think of Oracle CRM On Demand as a big website with a database behind it. Every screen that you view is a page on this website. This is a huge benefit to us when we consider the desire to embed analytics throughout the application. A little bit of HTML and, in some cases, JavaScript knowledge enables us to insert reports and dashboards throughout the interface. We are also able to embed navigation capabilities throughout the application.

The information and samples in the chapters that follow will guide you through embedding navigation and reports throughout Oracle CRM On Demand. That being said, it is impossible to anticipate every possible use of embedded analytics in Oracle CRM On Demand. I encourage you to explore and try new things, but always work toward meeting your company's reporting and business process needs. Exercise some restraint, and avoid feature creep in your implementations.

Access Control for Report Developers

Each user of Oracle CRM On Demand is assigned a role. Roles are part of the access control mechanisms that define the levels of access to records and screens in the application. The privileges identified in your user role control your ability to access and use the report development screens and tools. Each individual user has a single role, but a single role may be assigned to many users. Your system administrator is typically the individual who manages these role privileges. If you are unsure if you have the necessary access, ask your administrator to review the settings for your role.

Figure 1-1 shows a portion of the Role Privileges screen. There are eight Analytics privileges that affect your ability to access, create, and modify reports and dashboards in Oracle CRM On Demand. Most users will have at least some of these privileges, even if they are not responsible for creating or managing reports.

The Access All Data in Analytics privilege gives the user access to all data within reports. This bypasses all of the other access control mechanisms to expose data in reports that users may otherwise not have access to within Oracle CRM On Demand.

The Access Analytics Dashboards privilege gives the user access to the dashboards on the Dashboard tab within Oracle CRM On Demand. This privilege does not grant the user the ability to create or modify dashboards, only view them.

The Access Analytics Reports privilege gives the user access to the shared reports on the Reports tab within Oracle CRM On Demand. This privilege does not grant the user the ability to create or modify shared reports, only view them. Reports must be in a shared folder that is accessible to the user role. A user can have access to reports, but not have access to a specific folder. In this case, the folder and reports therein will not be visible to the user.

The Access Analytics Reports – View Prebuilt Reports privilege gives the user access to the prebuilt reports on the Reports tab within Oracle CRM On Demand. This privilege does not grant the user the ability to edit and create new reports based on the prebuilt reports, only view them.

Assign Privileges

Assign	Category	Privileges	Description
☑	Analytics	Access All Data in Analytics	Access all data in Analytics charts and reports.
☑	Analytics	Access Analytics Dashboards	Access the Analytics Dashboard.
☑	Analytics	Access Analytics Reports	Access the Analytics Reports tab.
☑	Analytics	Access Analytics Reports - View Prebuilt Analyses	View and execute prebuilt analyses and reports.
☑	Analytics	Analytics Scripting	Create Analytics Reports with views and data formats that can contain HTML or JavaScript.
☑	Analytics	Manage Custom Reports	Create, save, and publish customized Analytics charts and reports.
☑	Analytics	Manage Dashboards	Create, manage and design custom dashboards
☑	Analytics	Manage Personal Reports	Manage Analytics Personal Reports

FIGURE 1-1. *Analytics privileges for the user role*

The Analytics Scripting privilege grants the user the ability to embed HTML and JavaScript into reports. Some views in On Demand Answers are not available to the report developer unless this privilege is enabled. The narrative view, for example, accepts HTML and JavaScript code. While developers need this privilege to develop reports using HTML and scripting, users do not need this privilege to use reports containing these advanced features.

The Manage Custom Reports privilege grants the user the ability to create custom reports and save these reports into the shared folders so other users may access them. Without this privilege, a user may be able to execute and view custom shared reports, but cannot open the reports in On Demand Answers to modify them, nor can the user create a new custom report.

The Manage Dashboards privilege grants the user the ability to create, edit, and delete custom dashboards from the dashboard tab in Oracle CRM On Demand. The Manage Dashboards link appears on the Dashboard tab only if this privilege is enabled on the user's role.

The Manage Personal Reports privilege grants the user the ability to create custom reports and save these reports into their personal reports folder. Reports in your personal reports folder, named My Folders and appearing on the Reports tab as the My Analyses hyperlink, are not accessible to any users other than you.

Administrator Access Controls Required for Embedding Reports

Embedding reports and creating navigation links throughout Oracle CRM On Demand also requires that you have some administrative access to the application. As you will read later in this book, adding a report to a screen or adding a link from a detail screen to a report requires that you be able to create and edit fields, modify layouts, create and edit web tabs, and create and edit web applets. You may also be tasked with providing other users with access to these screens, which requires that you have even more administrative access rights. It is not unusual for your company's administrator to be the only person who has enough access to the application to perform the tasks described in this book.

There are six role privileges of note that affect a user's ability to perform many of the administrative functions described in this book. These privileges are enabled using the role privilege checkboxes shown in Figure 1-2.

- The **Customization: Layout Customize Application – Manage Dynamic Layouts** privilege gives you the ability to define and maintain dynamic layouts and assign those layouts to user roles. Dynamic layouts are record-detail screen layouts that change based on a value selected from the driving picklist field on the record.

- The **Customization: Layout Customize Application – Manage Homepage Customization** privilege gives you the ability to create and manage custom homepages and assign them to user roles.

- The **Customization: Layout Manage Homepage Custom Report Execution** privilege exposes the Displays The Execute Report Immediately check box on the homepage custom report wizard. Checking this check box forces the associated homepage report to run immediately when the homepage loads. If you leave this check box unchecked, a hyperlink is displayed in place of the report, requiring the user to click to generate the report. This is sometimes favorable when the homepage report takes a few moments to load and is not always needed by the user. Also, if the report is large and takes up a lot of screen space, the link may be desired to save space on the homepage screen. You may need to contact Oracle Customer Care to have this feature enabled.

☑	Customization: Layout	Customize Application - Manage Dynamic Layouts	Define Dynamic Layouts and assign them to Roles.
☑	Customization: Layout	Customize Application - Manage Homepage Customization	Create and manage custom homepages and assign them to Roles
☑	Customization: Layout	Manage Homepage Custom Report Execution	Displays the Execute Report Immediately check box on the homepage custom report wizard.
☑	Customization	Customize Application	Create custom page layouts, homepage layouts, change field names, modify field picklists, define cascading picklists, create custom fields and rename objects.
☑	Integration: Widgets	Embed CRM On Demand Widgets	Access CRM On Demand content outside of the CRM On Demand application.
☑	Integration: Widgets	Manage Custom Web Applets	Create, edit and publish custom web applets.

FIGURE 1-2. *Customization and integration role privileges*

■ The **Customization Customize Application** privilege is the key privilege that allows users to perform many common application customizations. This privilege allows you to create and edit custom page layouts, create and edit homepage layouts, change field names, modify picklist field values, define cascading picklists, create and edit custom fields, and rename objects.

■ The **Integration: Widgets Embed CRM On Demand Widgets** privilege provides you access to CRM On Demand content outside of the CRM On Demand application.

■ The **Integration: Widgets Manage Custom Web Applets** privilege gives you the ability to create, edit, and publish custom web applets.

Company Profile Setting Affecting Reports and Dashboards

In addition to the role settings, there are a couple of other places that affect data visibility in reports that you should be aware of. First, there is the Company Profile. The Company Profile may be modified by your system administrator. Second is the User Profile. Each user has a profile (record) in Oracle CRM On Demand that may be modified to provide specific data access within reports.

The Company Profile (Figure 1-3) has an Analytics Visibility section that contains three analytics visibility settings. The Reporting Subject Areas setting controls the data visibility of real-time reports. These are the reports built within the Reporting subject areas. The Historical Subject Areas setting controls the data visibility of the reports pulling data from the data warehouse. These are the reports built within the Analytics subject areas. The third setting has to do with the ability to see all records in reports. The Role-Based Can Read All Records setting (Figure 1-4), when set to Yes, enables a record-type specific setting of all record access based on the Record Type Access settings in the role definitions.

The options within the Reporting Subject Areas settings are Manager Visibility or Team Visibility. With the Manager Visibility option, users are able to view data in the reports owned by themselves and their subordinates. Essentially, they will see data owned by anyone in the user hierarchy below

FIGURE 1-3. *Company Profile: Analytics visibility setting*

them within their reporting line. With the Team Visibility option, users are able to view data in the reports that they have access to within Oracle CRM On Demand by virtue of their team membership. In other words, if Dave owns an account and Doug is on the account team for that account, Doug

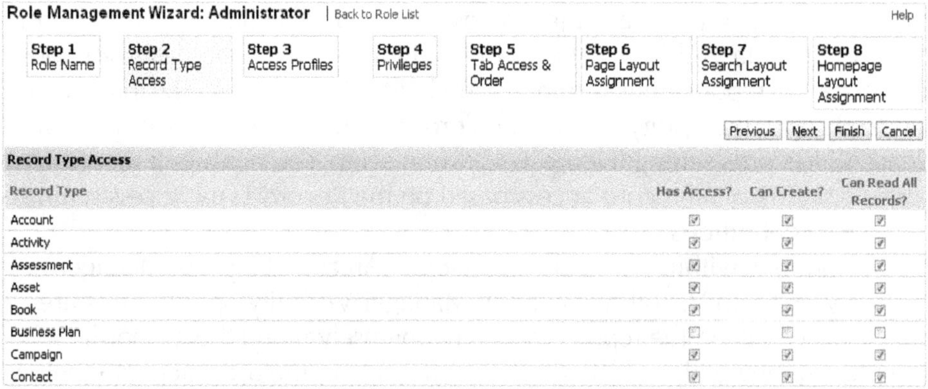

FIGURE 1-4. *Role Management Wizard: Record type access*

will be able to see that account on reports because of his membership on the account team.

One additional option is available within the Historical Subject Areas setting. The Full Visibility option allows users access to all data, regardless of ownership for historical (analytics) reports. This is useful when you are using the Analytics subject areas to report on company-wide trends and summary-type data that is not reported at the owner level. It is common to allow all users to see high-level sales data, for instance, at an aggregate level but to only provide access to the opportunity-specific details to the owners of those opportunities.

A user assigned to a role with the Access All Data privilege will be able to see all data in reports, regardless of the other visibility settings. Access All Data supersedes all other visibility settings.

User Profile Settings Affecting Reports

On the User Profile, you will find several fields that affect data visibility in reports. First, within the Key User Information section, the Default Analytics Look In setting allows you to set the default Book of Business User Book for the user's reports. Generally, this will be the user's own book. Book of Business is an optional feature. Your company may or may not have this feature enabled.

Also, in the Key User Information section, the Reports To field identifies each user's direct superior in the reporting hierarchy. This setting affects report data visibility when Manager Visibility is enabled.

Further down the User Profile, in the User Security Information section, you will find two fields that also appear on the Company Profile: Reporting Subject Areas and Historical Subject Areas (Figure 1-5).

When no values are selected on the User Profile, the data visibility settings on the Company Profile are used to determine which records should appear in a report for the current user. When User Profile settings are present, they will take precedence over the company settings.

Just like the fields by the same name on the Company Profile, the options available for Reporting Subject Areas are Manager Visibility and Team Visibility. The options available for Historical Subject Areas are Manager Visibility, Team Visibility, and Full Visibility.

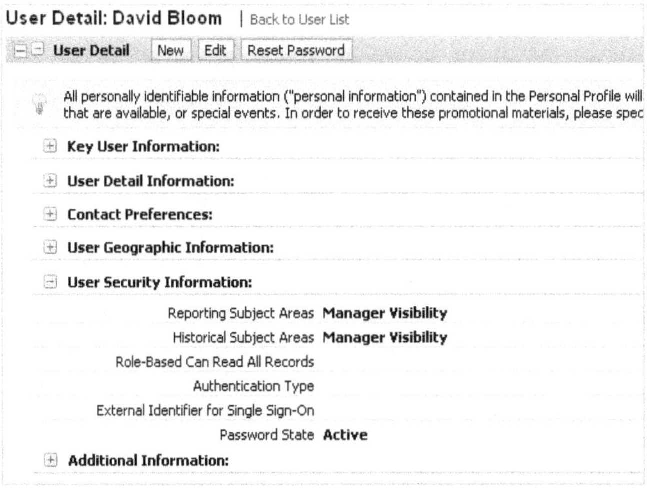

FIGURE 1-5. *User detail: User security information*

Introduction to Embedded Analytics

When you began your implementation of Oracle CRM On Demand, hopefully, you took the opportunity to examine your company's business processes and how users interact with your business data. If you did, you probably found that Oracle CRM On Demand was pretty close to what you needed to support your business with no configuration. After all, Oracle CRM On Demand is designed based on cross-industry most common business practices. Of course, you probably also found that some changes needed to be made to your business process or to On Demand or both to make everything match up just right for your unique business. The configurability of Oracle CRM On Demand is, after all, one of its best features.

As you compare your business process to your CRM application, you will find that there are points along the business process where a view of analytical data would prove useful or even critical to the success of a business task. You may have even developed some reports that provide this data. So far, everything I have described for you is common to nearly every implementation of Oracle CRM On Demand. Everyone configures the application at least a little bit, and everyone tends to develop some basic reporting to summarize business data. So far, none of this is terribly innovative when it comes to a CRM implementation, and this is where most implementations settle.

There is much more that can be achieved with a little creativity and some crafty report development, however, and that is where I hope this book benefits you. There are many places throughout Oracle CRM On Demand where reports and dashboards can be presented to the users. It is not necessary to send users to the Reports tab to navigate into the Shared Custom Analyses folder to find the report of interest and click the hyperlink to run the report. That process represents a minimum of four mouse clicks and screen changes to access a report and return to a record-detail screen in Oracle CRM On Demand. This is assuming that the report does not contain any column filter prompts that require input from the user to select specific records.

Consider some of the alternatives to forcing users to access the Reports tab to run a report. Take a typical sales scenario where a sales representative is viewing an opportunity record in Oracle CRM On Demand. This sales representative is about to call on her prospective customer and wants to review some sales information on the product associated with this particular sales opportunity to see the average length of product sales cycle and average sales price, and perhaps an analysis of why similar opportunities have recently closed successfully or why similar opportunities have been lost. This information is clearly very useful and will help the sales representative position the product with the potential customer.

We have a couple of options here for making this information available to the sales representative without forcing the user to go to the Reports tab, find the report, and select the product in the filter prompt. One option is to put a link to the report directly on the opportunity layout (Figure 1-6). The Web Link field would contain the URL for the report and could potentially pass values from the opportunity to the report automatically so that the report is filtered based on relevant column values.

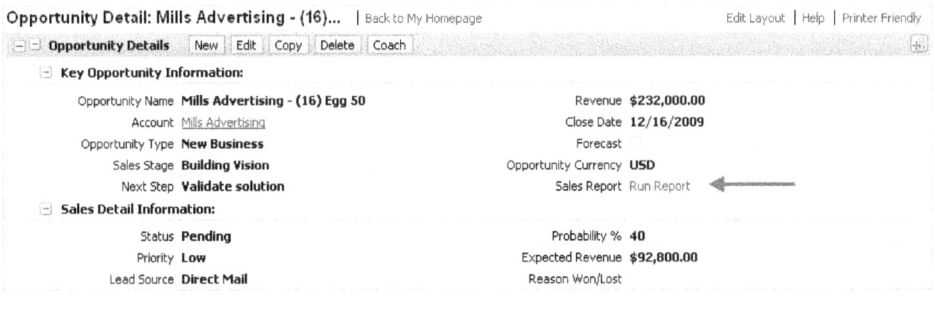

FIGURE 1-6.   *Web Link field on an opportunity screen*

Another option is to embed the report directly onto the opportunity detail screen by embedding the report inside of a custom web applet and expose the applet on the opportunity layout. This option also permits the passing of values from the opportunity to the report filters. This option actually requires no action from the sales representative to view the report, as it is embedded right on the opportunity screen.

This example illustrates the two classifications of embedded analytics that I describe in this book. First is the linked report. You may already be familiar with some methods for linking reports if you have done report development in Oracle CRM On Demand. Table 1-1 shows the many different types of links and where they can be embedded in the application.

Link Type	Link Action	Embedded Location
Navigation Link	Move from a report to another report	Column property within a report
Action Link	Move from a report to a detail screen	Column property within a report
HTML Hyperlink	Move from a report to a Detail or Edit screen	Data format of a record ID column
HTML Hyperlink	Move from a report to a Detail or Edit screen	Column formula formatted as HTML
Web Link	Move from Detail or Edit screen to a report or dashboard	Custom Web Link field on the record
E-mail Link	Create an e-mail message	Data format on an e-mail column
E-mail Link	Create an e-mail message	Column formula formatted as a mailto link
Dashboard Link	Dashboard screen to a report	Link/image object on a dashboard
Dashboard Link	Dashboard screen to a report	Report embedded as a link on a dashboard

TABLE 1-1. *Types of Linked Reports*

Providing links to and from reports requires that the user interact with the application in order to view the linked report or target of the link within the report. Many of these links can pass information from the source screen to the target screen. Linked reports still add a measure of convenience, and still require less interaction than navigating to the Reports tab and running reports.

The other method of embedding reports and dashboards is to display them directly in other screens throughout the application and, in one case, outside of the application. You may already be familiar with some methods for embedding reports if you have developed dashboards or selected reports for your homepage screens. These two common methods are just a couple of the places where reports can be embedded. Table 1-2 shows the many different methods of embedding reports.

You will notice that many of the methods for linking and embedding reports and dashboards rely on use of HTML. Oracle CRM On Demand is a browser-based application, so HTML as well as JavaScript and other Web languages feature prominently throughout Oracle CRM On Demand. As a user of Oracle CRM On Demand, you will rarely find occasion to need any sort of HTML coding skills. As a report developer, you may stick to basic reports and never encounter a situation where you need to use HTML.

Embedded Type	Embed Method
Report displayed on a dashboard	Dashboard Design - Report object
Report displayed inside another report	HTML in a narrative view
Report displayed on a record homepage	New Homepage report function
Report displayed on a Detail screen	Report embedded in a web applet
Report/dashboard displayed in a Web tab	Web tab HTML or URL
Report displayed in the Action bar	HTML in a global web applet
Display a report in a desktop widget	HTML in a widget or gadget application

TABLE 1-2. *Types of Report Embedding*

When you are linking and embedding reports, however, it is important to have some basic HTML knowledge. While this is not a book on HTML, later in this chapter I have included a brief primer on some basic HTML coding that you will find useful.

The Role of Embedded Analytics in Oracle CRM On Demand

Embedding a report is clearly a way to make reports more accessible to your users. Linking and embedding reports can reduce the number of clicks it takes your users to access report information. This is the primary, but not the only, role embedded analytics play in Oracle CRM On Demand implementations.

There are times when you may find yourself looking for a design solution that initially appears to have nothing to do with reporting. Interestingly, we very often find that reports provide a solution once we begin to exercise some creativity. Some examples of places I personally have used embedded reports to meet an odd business requirement include custom menus of links, replacing the Home tab with a custom tab full of reports, adding links to the Action bar, creating custom search screens, and more.

If we begin to think of reports as webpages that contain data from our CRM database, then making the leap from a standard tabular report to an embedded, seamless part of the Oracle CRM On Demand application is much easier to make. As you are designing your CRM On Demand application to fit the needs of your business and encounter a requirement to display information on the screen in a way that is different from standard CRM On Demand screens and applets, you may be able to meet that requirement using an embedded report. There is no checklist of requirements that embedded reports do or do not meet. You will develop a sense of what can and cannot be done as you enhance your report development skills. Meeting some of these more unique requirements does require some creativity and usually some advanced report development skills. The next chapter reviews some basic report development, with some tips for developing reports that you plan to embed on other screens. If you need assistance with more advanced report configuration, I recommend you explore my earlier books on the topic of CRM On Demand reporting.

The Importance of Planning

Earlier, I referred to the process of designing your Oracle CRM On Demand implementation and mapping business processes to the functionality of the application. Depending on the makeup of your implementation team, you may find it challenging to perform many of the embedding tasks after the individuals responsible for the configuration of the application have left the implementation team. Often, reporting is left to the end of the project and by the time you begin building all of the reports that you want inserted into the application, the individuals with the necessary configuration skills and access have moved on to work on other things. It is a good idea to map out the role of embedded reports early in the design phase so that the resources necessary are available. Also, I have seen many implementations where the user acceptance testing of the application occurs before the analytics tools are developed for the users. The opinion that reports are just an ancillary component of the implementation leads project teams to conclude that reports should not be included in user acceptance testing. Embedded analytics especially fall into the realm of something that users should test and approve prior to going live on Oracle CRM On Demand. If you consider that embedded analytics puts the reports in the hands of the users at specific points in the business process by offering links or embedding them right on the screen, it is clear that the reports are not ancillary, but are a critical component of the business process.

Also critical to the report development process are the requirements of the reports themselves and the configurations required to support them. There are many things to consider when planning your reports. If the report is going to sort through a large number of records, you will want to claim some indexed fields for the columns that you will query to populate the report. If you have some complex data access requirements, you will want to identify those prior to establishing the user hierarchy and visibility settings. If custom objects are going to come into play with your configuration, you will want to consider your reporting requirements prior to configuring the custom objects, or even determining which custom object you will use.

HTML You Should Know for Embedded Analytics

I hope by this point you are beginning to realize that embedding reports and dashboards in Oracle CRM On Demand requires a convergence of skills. In addition to report development skills, it is critical to have some application configuration skills. In addition to these two skill sets, you will find some basic HTML knowledge extremely useful. HTML stands for HyperText Markup Language. HTML is not a programming language, though you may hear people refer to HTML programming or coding.

You will find yourself using HTML on many occasions as you work to link and embed your reports in Oracle CRM On Demand. This section is intended to provide you with a primer on some basic HTML coding so that it is not completely foreign to you in the chapters that follow. If you are already an HTML programmer, feel free to move past this section.

HTML is a tag language. Basically, what that means is that you use tags to specify how text you type into the webpage should be treated by the browser. Some tags control formatting of the text and some tags control the functionality of the text. In the context of embedded analytics, HTML is used to create hyperlinks to and from reports, and is used to embed reports into a web frame on a screen within Oracle CRM On Demand.

Tags generally work in pairs. Most HTML commands include a start tag and an end tag, which dictate how the text should be formatted. For example, if the following string appeared in the HTML code of a page, the result would be "**Oracle CRM On Demand**" because the text is surrounded by bold tags:

```
<B>Oracle CRM On Demand</B>
```

The start tag for bold formatting is <B> and the end tag is </B>, so everything between the two tags in HTML appears in bold when viewed in a web browser. This is an example of text formatting in HTML. Other tags identify the structure of the page, create tables and frames, and add functionality. In the sections that follow I have described some of the most common HTML tags and provided some samples and their result.

Some HTML tags also take attributes. Attributes are additional commands or settings that work with the HTML tags to treat the text with particular optional formatting or functionality.

Structure Tags

Structure tags, shown in Table 1-3, identify parts of the page. You will not likely encounter too many places where you need structure tags. In a report narrative view, for instance, you will find that the header and footer structures are built into the view as separate fields when formatting the view. Structure tags do not generate any visible content on the webpage.

Basic Text Tags

Basic text tags, shown in Table 1-4, provide paragraph and font formatting. These tags control how text between them appears in the rendered page in the browser.

Function	Start Tag	Attributes	End Tag
Set document type to HTML	<HTML>	None	</HTML>
File header	<HEAD>	None	</HEAD>
File title	<TITLE>	None	</TITLE>
Comments	<!--	Insert comments into your HTML code by typing comments between these tags. Insert a space between the tags and your comments.	-->
Body	<BODY>	BACKGROUND="filename" BGCOLOR="color value" TEXT="color value" LINK="color value" VLINK="color value"	</BODY>

TABLE 1-3.   *HTML Structure Tags*

Function	Start Tag	Attributes	End Tag
Line Break	 or 	None	None
Paragraph	<P>	ALIGN="center/right"	</P>
Bold	<B>	None	</B>
Italic	<I>	None	</I>
Heading	<H1-6>	ALIGN="center/right"	</H1-6>
Font	<FONT>	FACE="font family" COLOR="color name" SIZE="number" Note: The FONT tag does not always affect text in On Demand, as view settings and style sheets generally take precedence.	</FONT>
Horizontal rule	<HR> or <HR />	WIDTH="pixels or percentage" NOSHADE	None

TABLE 1-4. *Basic Text Tags*

The following HTML code produces the result shown in Figure 1-7:

```
<HEAD>
<BODY>
<!-- This is an example of a simple webpage written with HTML using
Structure and Basic Text tags. -->
<H1 ALIGN="center">Sample HTML Page</H1>
<HR WIDTH="80%" ALIGN="center">
<P>HTML is relatively easy to learn. Using a few simple tags, you
can create <B>great</B> looking screens in Oracle CRM On
Demand.<BR>
Here's a tip for learning HTML:</P>
<BLOCKQUOTE><FONT FACE="arial">View the page source of some
webpages on the Internet and examine the HTML tags used. You can
learn a lot by imitating others.</FONT></BLOCKQUOTE>
<P>You can also find a lot of information on using HTML by
searching the Internet!</P>
</BODY>
</HEAD>
```

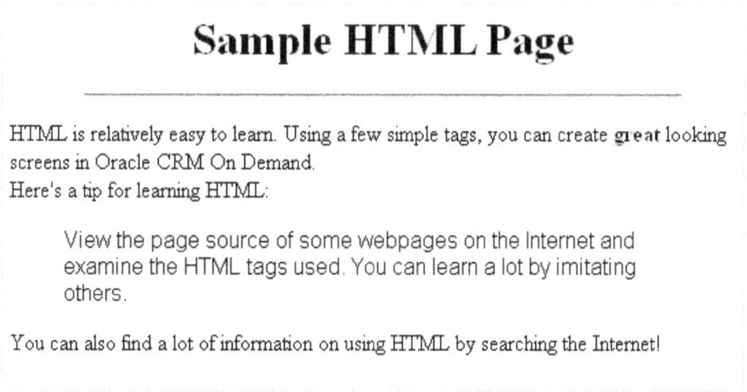

Sample HTML Page

HTML is relatively easy to learn. Using a few simple tags, you can create great looking screens in Oracle CRM On Demand.
Here's a tip for learning HTML:

> View the page source of some webpages on the Internet and examine the HTML tags used. You can learn a lot by imitating others.

You can also find a lot of information on using HTML by searching the Internet!

FIGURE 1-7. *Sample simple HTML page*

List Tags

List tags, shown in Table 1-5, allow you to format your text into lists. I have used list tags in the past to build custom reporting menus where I included links to reports as list items in the HTML. I am sure there are many other applications as well.

Function	Start Tag	Attributes	End Tag
Unordered (bulleted) list	<UL>	TYPE="disc/circle/square"	</UL>
Ordered (numbered) list	<OL>	TYPE="I/A/1/a/i" START="starting value"	</OL>
List item	<LI>	TYPE="I/A/1/a/i/disc/square/circle"	</LI>
Definition list	<DL>	None	</DL>
Definition term	<DT>	None	</DT>
Definition	<DD>	None	</DD>

TABLE 1-5. *List Tags*

Function	Start Tag	Attributes	End Tag
Anchor bookmark	\<A\>	NAME="bookmark name"	\</A\>
Anchor link	\<A\>	HREF="URL" NAME="bookmark name" TARGET="_blank/_parent/_self/_top"	\</A\>

TABLE 1-6. *Anchor (Link) Tags*

Link Tags

If you only learn a tiny bit of HTML, be sure that little bit includes link tags and frame tags. Table 1-6 lists the anchor tags. Anchors can be used in two ways: to create bookmarks within a page and to create links to other pages. You will see anchor tags featured prominently in Chapter 3 of this book.

Image Tag

The image tag inserts an image inside of your page. Image tags can be used when embedding reports when you want to insert an image on the screen that, when clicked, navigates the user to a report in Oracle CRM On Demand. Such a link with an image is demonstrated in the code after Table 1-7 and in Figure 1-8.

Function	Start Tag	Attributes	End Tag
Insert Image	\<IMG\>	SRC="filename" ALIGN="left/right" WIDTH="XXX" HEIGHT="XXX" ALT="image description"	\</IMG\>

TABLE 1-7. *Image Tag*

Click the image to the left to run the report.

FIGURE 1-8.   *Sample linked image*

```
<A HREF="/OnDemand/user/analytics/saw.dll?Go&Path=
%2fshared%2fCompany_XX1234-5XYZ6_Shared_
Folder%2fTop+10+Customers&Options=rfd&Action=Prompt" TARGET="_
BLANK"><IMG SRC="/OnDemand/user/analyticsRes/s_ondemand/images/
report_retailAudit.jpg" ALT="Report"></IMG></A> Click the image to
the left to run the report.
```

Table Tags

Table tags, shown in Table 1-8, allow you to present your HTML text inside
of tables. Links and images can be included in tables as well. I generally do
not use tables too often for embedded analytics, but have used the table tags
quite a bit within narrative views in my reports when I need to meet some
unusual layout requirements.

Inline Frame Tag

Inline frames are HTML windows inside of a webpage. Inline frames, or
iFrames, are used extensively when embedding reports and dashboards
throughout Oracle CRM On Demand. Table 1-9 shows the iFrame tag and
attributes. You will see iFrames in nearly every example featured in Chapter 4
of this book.

Function	Start Tag	Attributes	End Tag
Table	<TABLE>	ALIGN="left/center/right" BORDER="pixels" WIDTH="pixels or percentage" CELLSPACING="pixels" CELLPADDING="pixels" BGCOLOR="color value"	</TABLE>
Table row	<TR>	ALIGN="left/center/right" VALIGN="top/middle/bottom" BGCOLOR="color value"	</TR>
Table data	<TD>	ALIGN="left/center/right" VALIGN="top/middle/bottom" WIDTH="pixels or percentage" NOWRAP COLSPAN="number of columns to span" ROWSPAN="number of rows to span" BGCOLOR="color value"	</TD>
Table header	<TH>	ALIGN="left/center/right" VALIGN="top/middle/bottom" WIDTH="pixels or percentage" NOWRAP COLSPAN="number of columns to span" ROWSPAN="number of rows to span" BGCOLOR="color value"	</TH>
Caption	<CAPTION>	ALIGN="left/center/right" VALIGN="top/middle/bottom"	</CAPTION>

TABLE 1-8. *Table Tags*

Function	Start Tag	Attributes	End Tag
Insert inline frame	<IFRAME>	SRC="URL" ALIGN="left/center/right" FRAMEBORDER="1/0" HEIGHT="pixels or percentage" WIDTH="pixels or percentage" MARGINHEIGHT="pixels" MARGINWIDTH="pixels" SCROLLING="yes/no/auto"	</IFRAME>

TABLE 1-9. *Inline Frame Tag*

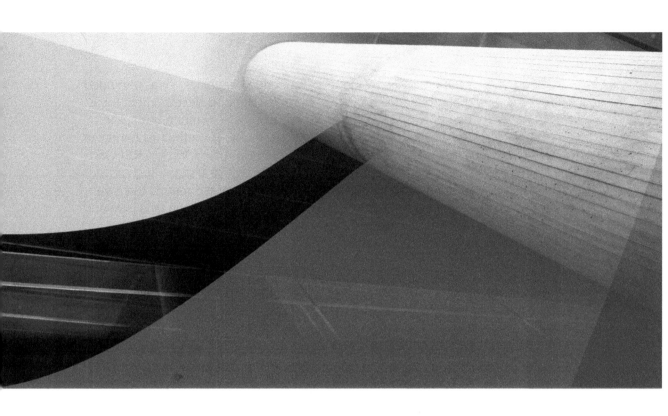

CHAPTER
2

Designing Reports
for Embedding

s I approached this topic of embedded analytics, I was reminded that embedded analytics is not just a report development topic or a system administration topic, but is very much both. The primary focus of this book, by necessity, is on the mechanics of actually embedding reports throughout your Oracle CRM On Demand application. This is primarily an administrative task in most cases. But just as important is the design and development of the reports that you plan on embedding into your application. First, there is the report development skill set, which I cannot assume you have already mastered, but some competency in this area will make the rest a bit easier. Next is the ability to design a report that visually works as part of a screen in the application. Ideally, we want our embedded reports to not appear to have just been stuck on the screen. We will want to spend some time working with the layouts and formatting of the report views so that they appear as natural on the screen as other elements.

This chapter covers the basics of report development and contains some advice on formatting your reports for linking and embedding. This is not meant to be a complete instruction manual on report development. If you need more information on report development, I encourage you to invest in a copy of my earlier book, *Oracle CRM On Demand Reporting* (McGraw-Hill/Professional, 2008).

Basic Report Development

The first step, and the most important, is planning your report. Determine the need for the report, the content that should be included in the report, how the report will be used, and when and where the users will access the report. Depending on the business environment you find yourself in, this step may require seemingly endless meetings with users, stakeholders, and management. If you are fortunate, the answers to these questions are blatantly obvious and do not require a committee to determine.

To begin building a report, you will access the Reports tab and click the Design Analysis link. This opens the Oracle On Demand Answers application in a new browser window. From this Getting Started window (Figure 2-1), you will select the subject area that you will build your report on. There are two sets of subject areas available here. Those on the left are the Analytics subject areas. These are tied to the Oracle CRM On Demand data warehouse and are considered historical subject areas because the data in reports built

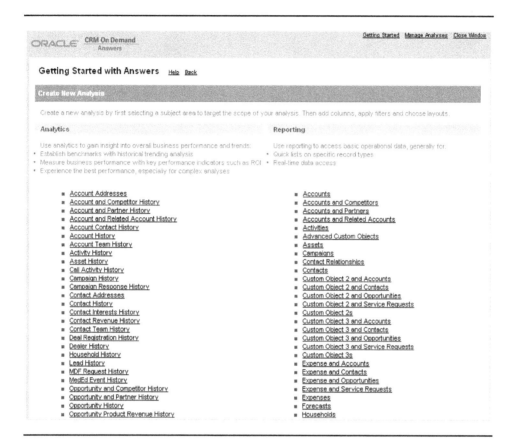

FIGURE 2-1.   *Oracle On Demand Answers – Getting Started screen*

on these subject areas is current as of the last Extract, Transform, and Load (ETL) process. The ETL is run nightly, so data could be up to 24 hours old.

The subject areas listed to the right are the reporting subject areas and are tied to the operational database. This is the same database in which your users are entering and modifying data. The data in reports built on reporting subject areas is real-time data and matches the data visible through the user interface of Oracle CRM On Demand.

Clicking one of the subject areas on this screen moves you to the On Demand Answers screen named Build And View Analysis (Figure 2-2). Let us take a moment to examine the Build And View Analysis screen. In the upper-left corner of the screen, you see the current subject area identified. Below the subject area name are all of the columns available within the

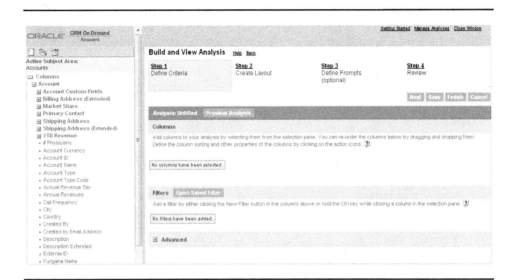

FIGURE 2-2. *Oracle On Demand Answers – Build And View Analysis screen*

subject area. You will find each column listed inside one of the folders in this columns list. The folder names generally refer to the source data table of the enclosed columns or the type of columns it contains. For instance, you will always find a Metrics folder in this list. The columns inside this folder are calculated metric columns.

The Preview Analysis button, located in the header below the step number indicators, allows you to have a look at your report in its current state. You will find yourself using this preview function frequently. When you click this button, a new window opens and generates your report. This is helpful as you experiment with different formatting and column arrangements.

In the main body of the screen, you see that we are on the first of four steps. As you move through the report development process, you will progress through these steps. Clicking the Next button moves you to the next step in the process. The Save button allows you to save your current report edits without closing the report. The Finish button also allows you to save the report, but then closes the report and takes you to the Getting Started screen. The Getting Started screen allows you to begin the development process on another report. The Cancel button allows you to exit from the current report without saving any changes you have made.

Clicking column names in the column list on the left side of the window adds the column to the report. The Columns section of the Build And View Analysis screen is where columns included in the report appear. You are able to configure exactly how you want the data in these columns to appear in your report.

Below the Columns section, you see the Filters section. This section shows all of the active filters affecting your report.

Adding, Removing, and Reordering Columns

When developing your report, you have the options of adding or removing columns from the report, reordering the columns that are in the report, or leaving the columns as they are and moving to the next step in the report design wizard to modify the views.

Once you locate a column that you want to add to your analysis, simply click the column name to add the column to the report. The column will appear in the Columns section of the Build And View Analysis screen. Each column has a table heading and a column heading. For example, if you add the Account Name column to your report, the top heading is Account and refers to the table name. The second heading on the column is Account Name, referencing the column name. You can change the order of the columns by dragging. Click the column heading and drag to move just that column. Click the table heading and drag to move all of the columns under that heading at once.

You may also find that you need to remove one or more columns from the report. Removing a column will eliminate the column from the report in its entirety, so all views referencing the column will be affected. To remove a column from your analysis, click the X button next to the column name.

Formatting Columns

Once you are happy with the columns in your report, you may want to format the data in the columns to suit your embedded report requirements. Before we get into formatting, notice the five buttons present on each column (Figure 2-3). The button on the left, which bears an icon of a hand, is the Column Properties button. The next button, which has the letters fx on it, is the Edit Formula button. The third button, with the image of a funnel, is the New Filter button. The red X button removes the column from the report, and the button next to the column name with the up and down

FIGURE 2-3. *Column buttons*

arrows is the Order By, or Sort, button. If you have trouble remembering what these buttons are, move your mouse pointer over the top of each one to see a tooltip displaying the button name.

In this section, I discuss the Column Properties and Sort buttons. Let us begin with the Column Properties. When you click the Column Properties button, the Column Properties window opens. As you can see in Figure 2-4, this window contains four tabs—Style, Column Format, Data Format, and Conditional Format. The intent of this book is not to exhaustively document report development, but to provide you with the information you need to link and embed the reports that you create, so we will take a quick look at each of these tabs.

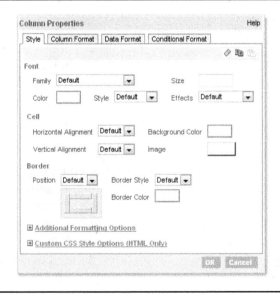

FIGURE 2-4. *Column Properties window*

Style Tab

The Style tab of the Column Properties window allows you to make decisions on the way the fonts and table cells appear on your report. The font settings available here allow you to set the font family, size, color, style, and effects. The default font is 10 point Arial, and the default color is black with regular styling and no effects. If you are planning to embed your report in a web applet to display it on a detail screen (this is described in Chapter 4), this is the place where you may want to do some formatting to make the report look as much like the rest of the screen as possible. You can find the current color settings by examining the active theme that your company is using. For more about themes, contact your system administrator or refer to online help.

Your font options are Arial, Arial Black, Arial Narrow, Courier New, Garamond, Lucida Sans Unicode, Microsoft Sans Serif, Times New Roman, Tahoma, and Verdana. If your company has a standard company font, you may want to select a font for your reports that adheres to this standard.

To change the font color, click the white box to open the Color Selector. There are 48 standard colors available here from which to choose. Alternatively, if you know the HTML color code for your desired color, you can enter # and the six-digit code in the field at the bottom of the Color Selector pop-up. This is true for all of the color options throughout Answers On Demand, enabling you to match your company colors precisely. You may also make your font bold, italic, or both using the Style field. The available effects are underlined and strikethrough.

Within the cell portion of the Style tab, you are able to apply horizontal and vertical alignment and add a background color to the cell. The default horizontal alignment is left for text fields and right for numeric data. The default vertical alignment is center. To apply a background color, click the white box next to Background Color, and select the desired color.

You can add single, double, or thick borders to one or more sides of your cell. You are able to select only one style of border for the cell. You apply the selected style to any side of the cell to which you want to add a border. To add a border, you can choose All from the Position field to apply a border to all four sides, or you can click the sides of the cell in the diagram below the Position field. The Color Selector beside Border Color works exactly like the others on this window and allows you to change the color of all borders applied to this cell.

Expand the Additional Formatting Options section, and you find fields that allow you to adjust the size of your column cell and the padding around the value within the cell. The Height and Width fields allow you to adjust the size of the cell by entering a desired size in pixels or by adding a percentage to make the column size relative to the size of the report table. A column width value of 50 is 50 pixels, while a value of 50% is half the width of the table. Adjusting the height of a column cell will affect cells across all columns because the table will adjust to the height of the largest cell in order to align the data in the table.

Cell padding provides space between the sides of the cell and the value in the cell. Adding padding around the cell values will override any specified height or width if the padding results in a larger cell size than the cell size setting. The inverse is also true. If the specified cell height and width settings result in a larger cell than the padding would cause, the height and width measurements apply.

There are three small icons in the upper-right corner of the Style tab. The left icon, an eraser, resets all of the style settings to the default values. The copy icon copies all of the style settings so you can access the column properties of another column and paste the settings to that column in one click.

These height and width settings can play a very important role in your design when considering the role of the report in the application and business process. The combination of your report design settings and your view properties on the report give you a great deal of flexibility in how reports appear on the screens and the amount of real estate that they occupy. I encourage you to experiment with different combinations of settings to achieve the layouts you are looking for in your embedded report.

Column Format

The Column Format (Figure 2-5) tab permits you to change the way values in the column repeat or group together across related rows of data, change the way the column heading and data react to a user's click of the mouse, or even hide the column from view.

To hide a column, select the Hide Column check box on the Column Format tab. The column will still be part of the report, and will affect the data on the report as if you are displaying the column.

If you want to change the grouping behavior of your columns, you can adjust the value suppression settings on the Column Format tab. To force values to repeat, select the Repeat setting in the Value Suppression section. You should make this change to all columns that you want to repeat.

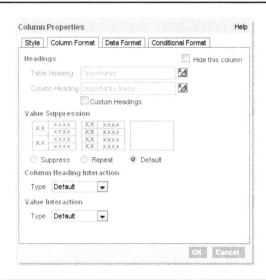

FIGURE 2-5.   *Column Properties window – Column Format tab*

Often, the default field name in Oracle CRM On Demand just does not fit your report. In such cases, you can change the headings to whatever pleases you by clicking the Custom Headings check box and typing the headings of your choice. The column headings appear in your reports. The table headings typically do not.

You can apply custom formatting to each of your headings. Click the Edit Format button, located to the right of each field, to open the Edit Format screen. This screen is exactly the same as the Style tab with the same options that you can apply to the table or column heading.

The final two fields on the Column Format tab allow you to adjust the interactivity of the column heading and the column value. The values in each of these fields are Default, None, Drill, and Navigate. Columns have different default interactivity behaviors depending on the column and the subject area you are using. If you know that you do not want any interactivity, select the None option. This will remove any default interactivity that may exist.

The drill interactivity allows users to drill down to see additional detail by filtering data on the value that the user clicks in the report. The navigate interactivity setting allows users to click a value in your report to navigate to another report. The report passes the value that the user clicks to the target report. When you select Navigate from the interactivity field, a new Select Navigation Target button becomes available. Clicking this button opens up two additional fields. These fields are the Target field, to identify the target report, and the Caption field, to provide the value that will appear in the pop-up menu that appears when there are multiple target reports available. To identify a target report, click the Browse button and navigate through the report folders to select the target report. Add a suitable caption to the Caption field if you are planning to add targets. If identifying only one target, the caption is not necessary. We will see this option again in the next chapter as we discuss the various methods for linking between reports and screens in Oracle CRM On Demand.

Data Format
The Data Format tab allows you to transform the data in the column into another format. This tab changes depending on the type of column. To change the format of the data in the column, click the Override Default Data Format check box. Doing so activates the fields on the tab, allowing you to select the desired format. This, too, plays an important role in certain types of links, and we will explore it in more detail in the next chapter.

Conditional Format
A common desire with reports is to highlight data that is below or above a particular threshold, or meets some other criteria that makes the data special in some way. Perhaps you want to assign a color to every salesperson and highlight their opportunity data in their particular color. Perhaps you want to call out service requests that have been open for longer than a week. You might even want to display some sort of graphic next to records that meet some requirement.

You can accomplish all of these things with conditional formatting. The Conditional Format tab in the Column Properties window, shown in Figure 2-6 with a few conditions already added, allows you to add formatting to column data that meets a defined condition. You access this tab for the column you wish to apply the formatting to. The conditions may be based on this column or on another column in the report.

To add a condition, click the Condition button on the tab, and select the column on which you want to base the condition. You will notice that you are able to select from any of the columns present in your report, including the column you are formatting. Upon selecting a column, the Create/Edit

FIGURE 2-6.   *Column Properties window – Conditional Format tab*

Filter window opens. Here, you select the condition and enter the value with which to compare the column data. Upon clicking OK, the already familiar Edit Format window appears for you to define the format for data meeting the condition. This formatting applies only to the column you are currently editing. If you want to apply a background color for an entire row, for instance, you will need to replicate your conditional formatting for each column.

You may continue to add conditions to the column to set formatting options for multiple conditions. When multiple conditions exist, the report evaluates the conditions beginning with the first condition in the list. When the report encounters data that meets a condition, it applies the conditional formatting and evaluates no additional conditions for that data cell. This means that the order of your conditions is very important.

After adding conditions to the Conditional Format tab, you can change the order of your conditions using the up and down arrow buttons next to each condition. Use these buttons to adjust the order to get the behavior you desire, remembering that for each row, the report evaluates the conditions starting with the first in the list, and once a matching condition applies, no further evaluation occurs for that row.

Sorting Columns

The Order By button is located to the right of the column name on step 1 of the Build And View Analysis screen. This button shows two arrows, one pointing up and the other pointing down. When the button appears this way, the column is unsorted.

Clicking the Order By button will toggle the sort direction. Click once for an ascending sort. The button now appears with a single green triangle pointing up. Click the button again, and the column changes to a descending sort. The triangle on the button now points down. Click the button a third time, and you return to the initial unsorted state.

The sorts are alphanumeric with numbers coming before letters. You are able to sort by multiple columns in your reports. The column you specify a sort on first will be the primary sort. The column you specify a sort on next will be your secondary sort. A small numeral 2 appears in the lower-right corner of the sort button, indicating that this column is the secondary sort. Likewise, the next column you set sort on is the tertiary sort and the button shows a small numeral 3 in the lower-right corner.

Filtering Report Data

Filtering your report data is easily the most important aspect of report design, and is a critical step when you are embedding reports that should display data relative to the record on which they appear. Applying filters to your report allows you to control which data you use to populate your report. Each filter is made up of three components: a column to filter, the value you want to use within the filter, and the condition that describes how the filter value is applied to the filter column. There are many of these conditions, called operators, available for your filters.

You can apply filters to one or more columns. These columns may or may not be included in your report results. Filters may be connected with an AND or an OR statement to affect the logic of how multiple filters work together. You can group filters together to create more complex filter logic. The options and possible combinations are plentiful and range from very simple to extremely complex.

Column Filters

The most common way to initiate the creation of a filter is by clicking the New Filter button on the column you intend to filter. Doing so opens the Create/Edit Filter window shown in Figure 2-7. You use this method to

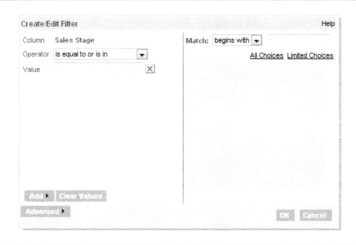

FIGURE 2-7.   *Create/Edit Filter window*

create a column filter on a column that you have included in your report. Of course, it is possible, and often desirable, to filter a report on a column not visible in the report. To open this window for a column without adding it to your report, hold down your CTRL key while clicking the column in the column list.

You will create most of your filters using the Create/Edit Filter window. On this window, you see the three basic components of the column filter. At the top of the window, you find the filter column. Below that is the Operator field, where you will select one of the operators for your filter. In the Value field you will enter the filter value, or select the value from the right to populate the Value field. With a text column, you have the option of displaying the possible values in a list and then clicking the value in the list to add it to the filter.

To display values to choose from, you have several options. Click the All Choices hyperlink to display all valid values for the current field. This often results in a lengthy list with multiple pages. Each page of this list displays ten values, and you are able to scroll through the pages using the number bar and arrows at the bottom of the window. If displaying all of your choices is a little too much, you have the option of clicking the Limited Choices hyperlink. The resulting list of values is dependent on any other filters already added to the report.

You may also perform a search on the valid values using the fields just above the All Choices and Limited Choices hyperlinks. Select "begins with," "ends with," or "contains" from the drop-down list, and enter a search value in the field to its right. Then click one of the links to see a list of values that meet your search criterion.

If you are modifying an existing report, you may have some filters that you want to modify or delete from the report. To re-open the Create/Edit Filter screen for a filter that is already on your report, click the Filter Options button to the right of the filter. This opens a menu. Select Edit Filter to open that particular filter and make changes to it. You will notice that you also have the option to cut or copy the filter. To remove a filter, click the Delete button to the far right of the filter.

Filter Groups

As you continue to add filters to the report, Answers On Demand ties these filters together with the AND statement. This is the default setting, but you are able to change the way your filters work together by clicking the AND link to change it to an OR connector between the filters. When you have the presence of both an AND and an OR connection between filters, the filters will automatically group together.

Continuing to click the AND/OR statements and ungrouping filters enables you to configure your filters to get the data you want in your reports. Often, report developers mistakenly think that it takes more than one report to collect different sets of data when perhaps a report with the appropriate groups of filters will do exactly what they need.

Predefined Filters

Answers On Demand also contains some predefined filters that you can use in your reports. To add a predefined filter to your report, click the Open Saved Filter button. This opens a window displaying the folder structure. Drill down into the filter folders by double-clicking the folders to display the contents. Select from one of the available filters, and click the OK button. Answers On Demand reacts by displaying the Apply Saved Filter window shown in Figure 2-8. This window shows you the location of the filter, and more importantly, the contents of the filter.

You also have a couple of options when applying this filter to your report. You may choose one or both of these options. The first option you have is to clear all existing filters before applying the filter. This might suit you if working on building filters for your report and, after trying a filter or

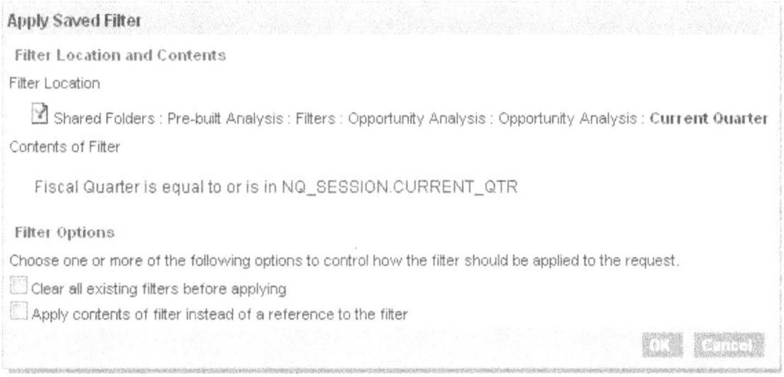

FIGURE 2-8. *Apply Saved Filter window*

two, determining that a prebuilt filter would better serve your purpose. Click the Clear All Existing Filters Before Applying check box, and when you add the predefined filter to your report, it replaces all other filters already on your report. Leave this option unchecked, and this filter appears at the end of the list of filters already on your report, if any.

The other option is to apply the contents of the filter instead of a reference to the filter. When a report references a filter, the saved filter is used when the report executes. Multiple reports can reference a single filter. When the contents of the filter are in the report, then the filter within the report is used and only that report uses the filter.

If your report contains the Active Filters view and the filter is rather complex, referencing a saved filter may be a preferable option just so the filter description looks a little better in your report result.

Filter Variables

To use a session variable in your filter, click the Add button on the Create/ Edit Filter window and select Variable. There is a small Variable submenu that contains the options of Session, Repository, and Presentation. Select Session from this menu to add the Session Variable field to the filter. The variable value can then be entered in the filter. A list of the most common session variables can be found in the online help.

While most variables are more appropriate topics for an advanced report development discussion, there is one session variable that is quite useful. The session variable REPLUSER returns the current user's sign-in ID, which is also the value of the User Email column in the Owned By User folder in the column list. An example use of this simple variable is to create a report that filters to records owned by the individual running the report.

Report Views

Step 2 of the Build And View Analysis wizard is all about the report views. Views are the visible elements of the report. Every report, when first created, contains a Title view and a Table view. Next, I provide a brief look into some of the primary views that typically appear in an embedded report. As you modify your reports, you will, at times, want to edit existing views, add views, or remove views from the layout. To add a view, you will click the Add View button on the Build And View Analysis – Step 2 screen (Figure 2-9) and select the type of view you wish to add to the report.

FIGURE 2-9. *Build And View Analysis – Step 2 screen*

Each view has three buttons in its upper-right corner. The first of these three buttons is the Format View button. This button opens the Edit Format window that allows you to set vertical and horizontal alignments for the view and to modify the border around the view.

The second button is the Edit View button. This button opens the Edit View screen for its view. This is where most of your view configuration takes place as described for the views below.

The third button is the Delete View button, which could be more appropriately named Remove View. Clicking this button does not exactly delete the view from the report. It does remove the view from the report layout, however.

Title View

When I am building a report that I plan to embed into an Oracle CRM On Demand screen, I typically remove the Title view from the layout. The title is useful when delivering as a normal report, but when embedded on a screen, the title tends to get in the way.

Clicking the Edit View button on the Title view takes you to the Edit View: Title screen, where you can adjust the settings for the title. On this screen you can modify the text that appears in the Title view of the report.

If you want to show a custom title rather than the saved report name, type the title you want to appear in the Title field and clear the Display Saved Name check box. If you add a custom title and do not clear the Display Saved Name check box, both will show on your report.

Place an image URL in the Logo field to include a logo or other graphic in your Title view. The logo is placed to the immediate left of your title text.

If you want a subtitle on your report that appears just below the title, add your subtitle text to the Subtitle field. Only text may be included in the Title and Subtitle fields.

It is often helpful to include information about when the report was run. In the Started Time field you have the option of selecting Date, Time, or Date And Time for display in your Title view. Of course, you may leave the default setting of Do Not Display if you do not want to display a date or time in your Title view.

Most of the Title view elements have their own formatting settings. You will find a Format Values button next to the Title, Logo, Subtitle, and Started Time fields. Within each of these Edit Title windows you are able to apply formatting to each individual element. The relative location of each element is fixed, though it is possible to change alignment, size, and colors.

As you adjust the settings for this and other views, you are able to see a preview of how the view will appear on your report. The Display Results section at the bottom of the edit screens usually updates automatically as you make changes to the view format. You may also refresh the preview by clicking the Display Results link. If you do not want to see the preview, you can remove the check mark from the check box. With some complex views, you may find it helpful to turn off the Display Results preview for better performance during your layout edits.

Table Formatting

Every report also starts with a basic Table view. The Table view includes all visible columns that you have included in your report. The formatting of the cell values in the Table view is based on the column format set on the columns in step 1. The header row displays the column name of each column. If you set a custom name for any columns on step 1, those custom names are applied on the Table view. The sort order set on step 1 also controls the sort order of the data in the Table view. If no specific sorts are set, the table sorts data in ascending order, beginning with the leftmost column.

Paging controls appear in the Table view if there are more than 25 records in the result set. These paging controls provide navigation buttons to page through the results one page at a time and buttons to display all pages and to return to the first page of results. The default location for these paging controls is below the table.

Click the Format View button on the Table view from the Step 2 screen, and the Edit Format window appears. Here you may set the horizontal and vertical alignments to adjust how the table appears on top of the base layer. Background color, borders, size, and padding are also available here, just like the other Edit Format windows we have used.

Clicking the Edit View button takes you to the Edit View: Table screen, where you can apply formatting to your table. By default, any format settings you made to your columns on step 1 are set here on the table. You can change your column formatting here using the same tools as on step 1. You can also add, move, and remove columns while editing your table, but it is usually easier to do these actions on the Step 1 screen.

Something you will see here that you did not see in step 1 is the Total By button on your nonmetric columns. This button has a sigma (Σ) on it and appears to be grayed out or unavailable. This simply indicates that you have not added a subtotal for that column. Click a column's Total By button to activate totaling and include a subtotal in all metric columns for each value in the column. The aggregation rules on the metric columns dictate how the values are aggregated. Once you have activated totaling on a column, if you click the Total By button again, you receive the pop-up menu with some additional settings.

Select None on the pop-up menu to remove the subtotals from your report column. The only location option for the subtotals is After, so you will always see a check mark next to After on this menu. Likewise, the Report-Based Total selection will have a check mark next to it by default. This indicates that the total will include only the values that appear in the report. In rare instances, you may try clicking this menu item to remove the check mark and see how it affects your report. I have never needed to do this.

Click the Format Labels menu item to apply formatting to the subtotal measurement label. The default value is the value in the column field followed by "Total." If you would rather have some other label for your subtotals, or if you want to apply a new format to the label cell in the table, click Format Labels to open the Edit Format window. The Edit Format window is one you should be familiar with at this point in the book, but you will see a new field here. The Folder field, while bearing a misleading name, is actually the measurement label, and entering a new value into this field changes your measurement label.

Click the Format Measure Values menu item to open the Edit Format window and adjust the format settings of the column subtotal values.

Moving up to the title bar above the columns, you will find another button with a sigma on it. This is the Grand Total button, and it functions and contains the same options as the Total By button. The difference here is that the Grand Total button adds a Total row at the bottom of your table.

To the immediate right of the Grand Total button you will find the Edit Table View Properties button. Clicking the Edit Table View Properties button opens the Edit View window. The lower half of this window should be familiar to you. The five fields at the top of this window are properties specific to the Table view.

The Paging Controls field allows you to control if and where the table paging controls will appear. Paging controls are the navigation arrows that appear in a Table view when the result data contains more than 25 records. You can choose to display the paging controls either at the top or at the bottom of the Table view. If you select Hide This Column in the Paging Controls field, the paging controls will not appear on your report. A word of warning on hiding the paging controls—if your result data contains more than 25 records and you have hidden the paging controls, your users will not be able to access the records beyond the first 25 unless you have changed the number of rows displayed on each page.

The Rows Per Page field is a freeform numeric field where you can set the number of rows to include on each table page. The minimum value accepted is one. This setting can come in handy when you are tweaking the layout of embedded reports and find that showing fewer rows in the table is more aesthetically pleasing and conserves valuable screen real estate.

The Display Column & Table Headings field gives you control over which values appear in the column headings and how they should appear. The default setting is to display only column headings. You may also choose to display both column and table headings. You can display the table headings as a separate row or before the column heading on the same row. The As Table.Column (where needed) option results in both the table name and column name appearing in the column heading for those columns that have the same name. You also have the option to not display a heading row on the table by selecting No Column Or Table Headings.

The Enable Alternating Row "Green Bar" Styling check box applies light green background shading to every other row in the table. This can enhance readability of tabular reports with many rows. My advice, if you want to use the green bar styling, is to be sure to set your table columns to repeat values rather than suppress values. This setting is on the Column Format tab of the Column Properties window

The Enable Column Sorting In Dashboards option activates column sorting in your table. Users will be able to click a column header to sort the data by that column. This feature works very much like the column sorting in a record list.

The next two tools on this view affect only the way your table appears in the preview on the Edit View: Table screen. The Refresh button refreshes the data in the table. Do not use the browser refresh while editing your table. Doing so will return you back to step 1 of the Build And View Analysis screen, and any changes are lost.

The Display Selector allows you to control what displays in the preview on the Edit View: Table screen. By default, the display includes header toolbars with results. You may choose to display header toolbars only or results only by selecting a different value from the Display field.

Chart Views

On step 2 of the Build And View Analysis screen, you will find the Add View button just above the preview of your report views. Clicking this button opens a menu of views that you can insert into your report. One of these options is Chart. Selecting Chart from the Add View menu will insert a basic chart into your report. You will also see among the options in the Add View menu two other chart views that I will describe in this section. Those are the Gauge view and, under the Advanced submenu, the Funnel Chart view.

Whether you are adding a new chart or editing an existing chart, you will find yourself on the Edit Chart View screen. Here, the buttons and picklists in the header bar above the chart allow you to set the properties and chart type for your Chart view. These charting controls are similar across all chart types.

In the Graph field, select the form of chart that you want to insert into your report. Your options here include Area, Horizontal Bar, Bubble, Vertical Bar, Line, Line Bar Combo, Pareto, Pie, Radar, Scatter, and Step. When you select a value from the Graph field, the chart preview updates to display the selected graph with the current settings.

The Type field varies slightly depending on the value you have selected in the Graph field. In most cases, you can choose between a three-dimensional appearance and a two-dimensional appearance for your chart. The bar style graphs (horizontal, vertical, and line bar combo) have added options for two- and three-dimensional stacked types. The Scatter graph type values are Scatter and Scatter With Lines. When you select a value from the Type field, the chart preview updates to display the chart with the selected type.

Finally, the Style field allows you to select shapes and shading formats depending on the graph selected. Not every graph has options available in the Style field.

The first button on the title bar is the General Chart Properties button. The icon for the General Chart Properties button is similar to the Column Properties icon you are accustomed to seeing on the columns in step 1. Click this button, and the General Chart Properties window opens.

On the General Chart Properties window, you can format the title, data labels, and chart size. By default, your chart will not have a title. To add a title, click the Custom Title check box and type your desired title in the Title field. Click the Text Format button next to the Title field to set the font family, color, style, and font size for your title on the Text Format window.

In the Data Labels section of the General Chart Properties window, you can set how and when data labels will appear in your chart. The default setting for showing data labels is to show your data labels on rollover. This means that the amount reflected by an element on your chart displays whenever the mouse pointer moves over that element. You may click the Text Format button next to your chosen data label setting to modify the font appearance.

Click the Override Default Data Format check box if you want your values to display in a different format. Your choices are to display your numbers as numbers, currency, or percentages. Make this selection in the Treat Numbers As field. You may also adjust the format for negative values in the Negative Format field. Finally, you are able to select the number of decimal places to include in the data values and choose to use a thousands separator within the values.

If you have identified a new data format on the columns already, that selected format is used by default. You can change that format using the fields described earlier.

The Size section of the General Chart Properties window (Figure 2-10) allows you to adjust the overall size of the chart in your report. You may enter the height and width in points to adjust the chart size, or you can use the sliders beneath and to the right of the chart preview to set the chart size. The benefit of using the Height and Width fields is that you can set the size

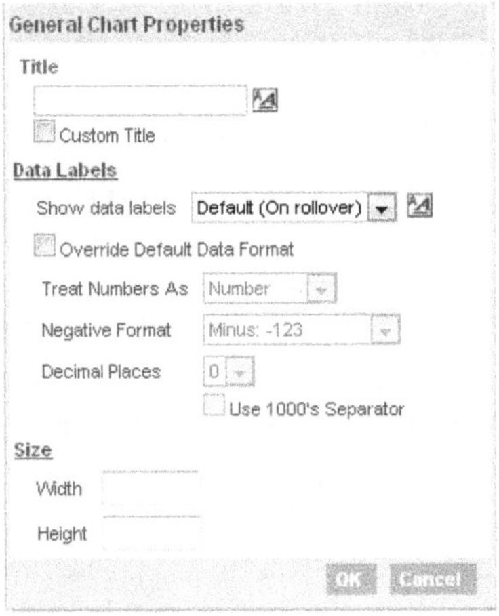

FIGURE 2-10. *General chart properties*

precisely and beyond the limits of the sliders. Using the sliders, the width range is 90 to 810 points and the height range is 60 to 540 points.

The next button on the title bar is the Axis Titles And Labels button. This button opens the Axis Titles & Labels window (Figure 2-11), which contains two or three tabs, depending on the chart type. The Left tab (and Right tab for some charts) allows you to configure the title and label formats of the vertical axis. The Title section controls the axis title, which will default to the column name for the values displayed along that axis. You can change the title by clicking the Custom Title check box and typing a new value in the Title field. Format the title's appearance using the Text Format button next to the Title field.

The Labels section of the Left or Right tab contains a series of fields that allow you to format the scale labels. The Display Scale Labels check box permits you to turn the labels off by removing the check mark. If you want to keep the labels, you can format their appearance by clicking the text format button next to the check box field and the remaining check boxes and fields on the tab.

The fields that appear on the tab depend on whether your scale labels are text or numerical. When formatting either text or numeric scale labels, you can choose to rotate those labels. Click the Rotate Labels check box, and select the angle you want to use. Your options are between 90 and –90 degrees.

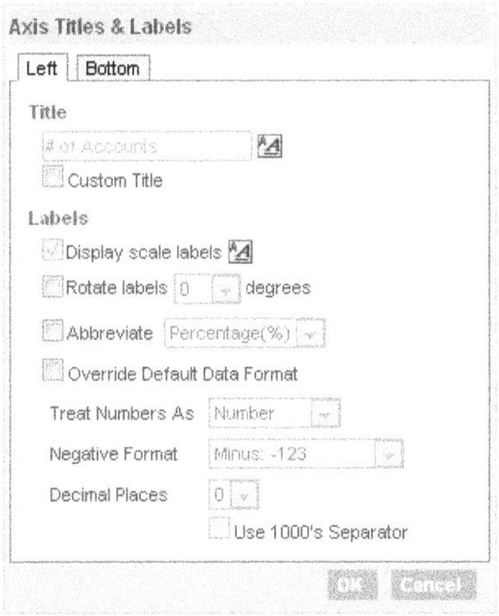

FIGURE 2-11.   *Axis Titles & Labels window*

Two settings for text scale labels are options for staggering the labels or skipping labels if necessary. These two check boxes appear on the tab only when the scale labels are alphanumeric. When your scale labels are numeric, you have the option of abbreviating the number in percentages, thousands, millions, billions, and trillions. Simply click the Abbreviate check box and select the abbreviation type. You can also override the numeric data format by clicking the Override Default Data Format check box and then identifying how you want to treat the numbers, the negative format, and the number of decimal places. You also have the option of using the thousands separator.

The Bottom tab also has a Title section and Labels section for modifying the title and scale labels of the bottom axis. The options here are exactly the same as the Left tab for an alphanumeric data type.

The next button is the Axis Scaling button. This button takes you to the Axis Scaling window (Figure 2-12), which will have one or two tabs, depending on the type of chart. A line bar combo, for instance, has a scale on the left vertical axis and on the right vertical axis. Both the left and the right tab on the Axis Scaling window contain the same fields, but may have different settings within those fields.

The Axis Limits section in the Axis Scaling window allows you to control the value range for your chart axis. Within the Axis Limits section, you have

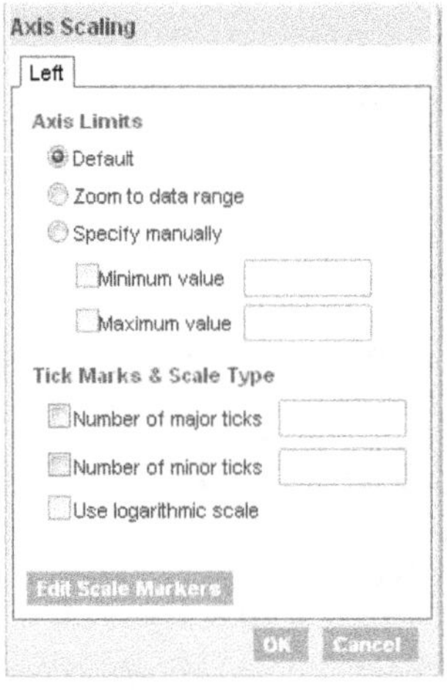

FIGURE 2-12. *Axis Scaling window*

three choices. You can keep the default scale, which is determined dynamically based on the upper and lower numbers within the data you are charting. You can also zoom to the data range, which is similar to the default scale, but adjusts the axis scale so that the data represented in the chart occupies roughly three-quarters of the scale. The third option is to specify the scale manually. This is where you risk skewing the perception of the data significance. Upon selecting the Specify Manually option, you use the Minimum Value and Maximum Value check boxes and fields to manually set the upper, lower, or both thresholds of the chart.

The next section on the Axis Scaling window, Tick Marks & Scale Type, allows you to adjust the number of horizontal major and minor ticks present on your axis scale. The easiest way to figure out how many ticks you should insert is to take the top number of the scale and divide by the size of each major section of your scale and then add one. You may also specify the number of minor ticks. This is the number of ticks between your major ticks. To determine the number of minor ticks, divide the span between major ticks by the size of your desired minor tick and then subtract one.

The final check box on this window changes your scale from a standard scale to a logarithmic scale. The logarithmic scale of measurement uses the logarithm of a physical measurement rather than the measurement itself. Logarithmic scales have specific applications—usually with data sets that have very large ranges or some statistical analyses.

Click the Edit Scale Markers button on the Axis Scaling window to open the Scale Markers window (Figure 2-13). Here you can add markers in the form of lines or ranges to your chart. To add a marker, click the Add button. Give the marker a name in the Caption field. This caption will appear in the chart's legend. Select the type of marker, either Line or Range, in the Type

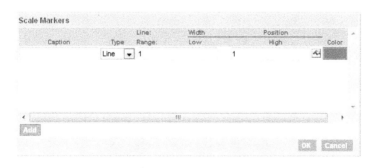

FIGURE 2-13.   *Scale Markers window*

field. The purpose of the next two fields depends on your selection in the Type field.

For a line marker, the first field is the width of the line in points. The second field identifies the position of the marker line on your axis scale. The Advanced Options button, located to the right of the position field, opens the Advanced Options window that allows you to use a column value to position your marker line. For instance, if you have included a column that calculates an average value, you could use that column to locate your marker in order to identify the average value on your chart. If you identify a column for your marker that contains different values across the rows of your table, the marker will appear at the first value that it encounters in the table. Sorting your data may affect which record determines the marker position. You can also set the color for your marker line by clicking the color box and selecting a new color from the palate, or entering an HTML color code and clicking OK.

For a range marker, the first field identifies the low end of the range and the second field identifies the high end of the range. The advanced options for each of these fields is the same as I described for the line marker. A range marker applies shading on the background across the width of your chart between the marker amounts specified.

To the right of the Axis Scaling button is the Additional Charting Options button. This opens the Additional Charting Options window. This window contains four tabs, each dedicated to a different element of your chart.

The first tab, shown in Figure 2-14, is the Grid Lines tab. Here you can change the color of the major and minor grid lines. Clicking the Override

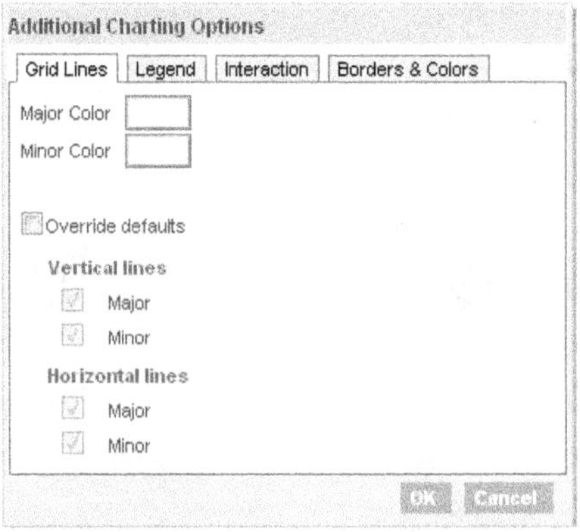

FIGURE 2-14. *Additional Charting Options – Grid Lines window*

FIGURE 2-15. *Additional Charting Options – Legend window*

Defaults check box enables the check boxes on the tab that allow you to disable major, minor, vertical, and horizontal grid lines.

The next tab, Legend (Figure 2-15), provides some control over if and where your chart legend appears. You can choose to display your legend on the right (default), left, top, or bottom of your chart. You may also select None in the Location field to remove the legend from your chart. The format button, located next to the Location field, provides some typical text-formatting controls. You may also indicate the number of columns that your legend should contain if there are enough items in the legend to spread the items across more than one column.

The Interaction tab (Figure 2-16) allows you to select the type of interaction that will occur when a user clicks part of the chart. The default setting is Drill. You may disable interactivity or set up a navigation path to another report.

The fourth tab, Borders & Colors (Figure 2-17), allows you to set a color for your chart's background, text, and border. To change the color for any of these, click the color box next to its label and select a new color from the palate, or enter an HTML color code. The border and background encompass the entire chart, including the title and legend. The text elements that the color setting affects are the axis titles.

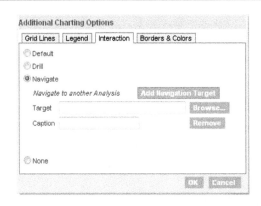

FIGURE 2-16. *Additional Charting Options – Interaction tab*

The Format Chart Data button opens the Format Chart Data window (Figure 2-18), where you can format the appearance of your chart data elements. You can specify the color and style for each series and each chart component. This window appears differently for different charts. The Format Chart Data window for basic bar charts is the least complex. To change the color of the bars in your chart, clear the Use Default check box for the series position you want to recolor, and then click the color box and select or enter your new color.

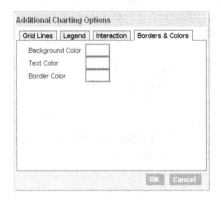

FIGURE 2-17. *Additional Charting Options – Borders & Colors tab*

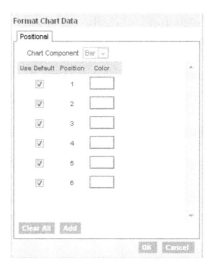

FIGURE 2-18.   *Format Chart Data window*

With the Format Chart Data window for a line chart, you have the same coloring settings plus some additional settings for the line type and width. You have the option of choosing a plain line (default), dotted line, dashed line, or the dash-and-dot line for each series. You can set the width of your line from zero to six points. Lines may also have symbols at each data point. You can select the symbol shape from the Symbol Type field. Your choices of symbols are square, triangle, round, diamond, and a plus sign. You can also choose to turn the symbol off.

The Line Bar Combo chart uses both the line and bar versions of the Format Chart Data window. The Chart Component field allows you to switch between formatting your lines and your bars.

The Format Chart Data window for the Pareto chart combines the line and bar formatting fields onto one screen, allowing you to set the color of the bar with the upper color box at each position and the line formatting with the lower set of fields at each position.

With a pie chart, you have the option of exploding one of the chart wedges out of the circle. With a bubble chart, you have the additional option of making the bubbles appear three-dimensional or two-dimensional. Regardless of the chart type, one final common element on the Format Chart

Data window is the Clear All button. Any time you feel you have gone a little too far with your formatting, click the Clear All button to reset all options back to their default values.

With the bubble, line bar combo, and pie charts, you are able to make additional special formatting changes by clicking the Advanced Properties button. On the bubble chart, this button opens the Chart Type Special window containing a slider for adjusting the bubble size percentage. On the line bar combo, the Chart Type Special window contains a single check box that allows you to synchronize the line and bar axis scales. Finally, the pie chart's advanced properties permit you to format the data values as a percentage of the total or the actual value represented by each wedge. You can also define what information is included in the data label. You can display the value only, the name only, or both the name and value.

Each Edit view for charts contains a series of check boxes that you use to indicate which columns to include in your chart and where the column data should appear. Depending on the chart type, you will see a column of check boxes beneath icons representing chart elements. You will have between two and five columns of these check boxes. Some charts also allow you to identify if and where to apply measure labels. The specific requirements of each chart type are described in the following section.

To the right of these check box controls, you have a preview of your chart. This preview may update automatically as you make changes, but you will find that you need to click the Redraw button at times to refresh the preview. If you ever feel like you have gone too far with your chart formatting, you can click the Restore Default button to return to the default format for the current chart.

Review of Chart Types

Selecting the most appropriate charts for your report will make your report more effective and acceptable to your users. The point of an embedded report, after all, is to deliver analytical information to the user in a seamless and meaningful way. Keeping your embedded reports as simple and noninvasive as possible will help users successfully complete business processes. Nothing accomplishes this better than a well-placed chart.

Area An area chart displays quantitative data by filling in an area under a series line. Area charts are good for showing the total of two or more quantities over a series of time, for instance, while representing the individual quantities that make up that total.

The area chart requires you to identify columns for the bottom and left axes. In order to populate your area chart, you need to identify the column by which to segment the data in the chart. The values from this column appear along the bottom axis. Identify this column by selecting the column's check box beneath the bottom axis icon. This is usually a nonmetric column.

Next you will identify one or more metric columns to include on the left (measure) axis. Select the Measure Labels check box under the legend icon, and you get a nice area chart with different color areas for each metric and a legend that identifies the metric associated with each color.

Horizontal Bar   A horizontal bar chart displays quantitative data represented by horizontal bars extending from the left axis. The chart displays series as sets of horizontal bars grouped by category. Metric values are represented by the length of the bars as measured by the bottom axis. Category labels appear on the left axis. You will normally use a bar chart when you want to compare values between categories.

There are two types of horizontal bar charts. The standard horizontal bar chart represents each metric as an individual bar. The stacked bar chart displays all metric series stacked into a single column for each category.

The horizontal bar chart requires you to identify columns for the bottom and left axes. You must identify the column by which to segment the data in the chart. The values from this column appear along the left axis. Identify this column by selecting the column's check box beneath the left axis icon. This is usually a nonmetric column.

Next you will identify one or more metric columns to include on the bottom axis. Select the Measure Labels check box under the legend icon if you want the legend to identify what the different colored bars represent.

You must identify at least one column for the measure axis, and you cannot set your measure labels to the measure axis. If you fail to designate a column for the left axis, the report will use a combination of all unused columns on the left axis.

Bubble   A bubble chart displays data series as a set of circles (bubbles). Metric values are represented by the position of the point in the chart corresponding to the left and bottom axes, and a third measurement affects the size of the bubble. Categories are represented by different-colored bubbles in the chart. There is only one type and style of bubble chart.

In order to display meaningful data in a bubble chart, you will need to identify a category, represented by the diagonal axis, or chart area. The location of the bubble for each value is based on its relationship to the metric values on the bottom and left axes. The fourth element is size. A metric value assigned to this element in the bubble chart determines the size of each point in the chart. Adding a column to the legend causes the bubble chart to show different color-coded series of bubbles.

Vertical Bar   The vertical bar chart is the default chart type. Every time you add a Chart view to your report, you will always start with a vertical bar chart. A vertical bar chart displays quantitative data represented by vertical bars extending from the bottom axis. The chart displays series as sets of bars grouped by category. Metric values are represented by the height of the bars as measured by the left axis. Category labels appear on the bottom axis. You will normally use a bar chart when you want to compare values between categories.

As with its horizontal counterpart, there are two types of vertical bar charts. The standard vertical bar chart represents each metric as an individual bar. The stacked bar chart displays all metric series stacked into a single column for each category.

The vertical bar chart requires you to identify columns for the bottom and left axes. You must identify the column by which to segment the data in the chart. The values from this column appear along the bottom axis. Identify this column by selecting the column's check box beneath the bottom axis icon. This is usually, but not necessarily, a nonmetric column.

Next you will identify one or more metric columns to include on the left (measure) axis. Select the Measure Labels check box under the legend icon if you want the legend to identify what the different-colored bars represent.

You must identify at least one column for the measure axis, and you cannot set your measure labels to the measure axis. If you fail to designate a column for the left axis, the report will use a combination of all unused columns on the bottom axis.

Line   A line chart displays categories of data as points connected by lines. Measure values along the left axis determine the height of each point along the line. The line contains a point for each value in the category series displayed along the bottom axis. You will typically use a line chart to compare values over time.

For each measure column you identify on the left axis, your chart will display a line of a different color. You may also manually set the line colors on the Format Chart Data window, perhaps even make all of the lines the same color, but different types. You are required to designate at least one column on the left axis. The bottom axis and legend elements are optional, but at least one is needed to display anything meaningful in your line chart.

Line Bar Combo   The line bar combo chart, as you might expect, is a combination of the vertical bar chart and the line chart, with all of the options available in each. The bar chart portion of the chart displays quantitative data represented by vertical bars extending from the bottom axis. The line chart portion displays another metric as points connected by lines with the measure values scale along the right axis determining the height of each point in the line. The line contains a point for each value in the same category series as the bar chart displayed along the bottom axis.

The line bar chart permits you to show a relationship between metric series, even when the scales are vastly different. This strategy is often used when comparing two different data types to identify correlations between them. Your bars may represent numeric data, for instance, while the line represents currency data.

You still have the option of a standard vertical bar chart representing each metric as an individual bar or a stacked bar chart displaying all metric series stacked into a single column for each category. The line bar chart requires you to identify columns for the bottom and left axes. You must identify the column by which to categorize the data. The chart will use this column to segment the data in the chart for both bar and line portions along the bottom axis. This is usually, but not necessarily, a nonmetric column.

Next you will identify one or more metric columns to include on the left (measure) axis. If you only select one column, the resulting chart will appear as a line chart, even if you select the column under the left axis. If you select two columns on the left axis and none on the line element, the chart will display the first column as a line and the second as bars. Of course, you can designate which columns to show as lines and which to show as bars by clicking the column's check box under the icons according to your preference.

Pareto   A Pareto chart is a special line bar chart where the bars are arranged in descending order according to value. The bar on the far left is the largest and the bar to the far right is the smallest. The line shows a running aggregate of the percentage of the total so that the line always ends at 100 percent in the upper-right corner of the chart. The steeper the angle of this line, the more evenly spread are the values across the segments in your chart. A relatively flat line would indicate that one segment contains a vast majority of the value in the data set.

Pareto charts are often used to analyze the frequency of issues. If you do any work in quality control, you are very likely to have seen many Pareto charts in action. To set up a Pareto chart in Oracle CRM On Demand, you will need to identify the bottom axis—the segmentation of your data—and the left axis—the measure to evaluate. You are only able to measure one column at a time on the measure axis. If you select more than one column on the left axis, the chart will reflect only the first measure column it encounters. The scale on the left axis is based on the column values. The right axis will always be 0 to 100 percent.

Pie   Perhaps the most popular multicolored circle in the charting world, the pie chart is a common choice for showing proportions within data. Despite its popularity, the pie chart is actually not terribly useful. It is difficult to compare multiple segments within a pie chart or compare values across multiple pie charts. The size of the wedges in a pie chart are proportional within that single chart according to data values, but the size of the pie can be misleading across multiple charts.

Your pie chart requires you to identify two elements for your chart. The column you choose for the legend element will determine the number of wedges present in your pie chart. The other element is the measure, and the column you select for this element will determine the size of each wedge. Unlike bar charts and line charts, the scale for a pie chart is not obvious. The data is represented only by a wedge, and if your chart includes several similar-sized wedges, it would be difficult to determine at a glance which wedge is bigger. In my opinion, pie charts are most effective if there are no more than four or five segments.

If you want to deliver more detail, you can display the percentages or actual values using the Advanced Properties button. In the General Chart Properties window, set the chart to always show the values or show them when the user moves the mouse over a wedge. Another option for drawing the user's attention to a particular portion of the data is to explode one of the wedges out of the chart. Do this by clicking the Explode Wedge option for the segment on the Format Chart data window.

Radar   The radar chart, also known as a spider or spider web chart, is an interesting and informative chart for comparing multiple attributes of several different values on the same scale at a glance. For instance, suppose you have a team of six salespeople, each with a goal of 20 sales per month. With the radar chart, you can graphically represent each salesperson's goal, current number of opportunities, and number of wins as shaded areas on the chart. Zero on the scale is the center of the chart. The radar chart seems to combine the benefits of bar charts and pie charts.

To configure your radar chart, you identify the column whose value will occupy the points around the outside of the chart. These are the segments into which you will organize the values. You can then identify one or more columns for the measures. Each column is assigned a color and appears as a shaded area inside the radar.

On the down side, you are rather limited in regard to the customization of a radar chart. You cannot change the grid lines, for instance. You also have no control over the scale and cannot add a scale marker in the normal fashion. You can, however, add a new column to your report and hard-code a value to force a marker into the radar chart.

Scatter   The scatter chart plots data points on a grid, and is a perfect solution for recognizing trends in a large data set. Correlations between two different metrics become clear on a well-designed scatter chart. We see correlations on a scatter chart as a cluster that moves from the lower left to the upper right of the chart. In other words, as one metric increases, so does the other metric. A negative correlation would show as a cluster arranged roughly from the upper left to the lower right. As one measure increases, the other measure decreases.

Configuring your scatter chart is similar to configuring a bubble chart, only the element of size is not present. Assign your two measure columns to the bottom and left axes. Assign the segment column—the column to which the two measures are attributed—to the body of the chart represented by the diagonal line icon on the Edit View screen. The Measure Labels option is not a valid part of a scatter chart, as the segment values are not identified by different-colored dots.

The sizing of the scatter chart affects its interpretability more significantly than any other chart. If you adjust the height or width of the chart so that one is much larger than the other, the cluster of dots appears skewed, as they are smashed either vertically or horizontally.

Step   A step chart is quite similar to a line chart. The step chart plots the data point on the chart grid and connects these points with straight lines, just like a line chart. The difference here is that the data points are connected by horizontal and vertical lines. The data points are actually plotted as horizontal lines between two segments. The segments on the bottom axis are assigned to the space between the vertical grid lines rather than a point on the grid line. The end of each horizontal line is connected to the start of the next horizontal line by a vertical line.

If you sort your data by the measure value, your step chart becomes quite easy to read and the length of the lines gives some insight into trends within the data. For instance, long horizontal lines that span multiple segments indicate that several segments contain equal measures. Long vertical lines indicate either a large jump or drop in the data, depending on how you sorted the values.

This type of chart seems to draw a staircase, lending to its name, and irregularities in the lengths of lines make variations in the data quite obvious. Like a line chart, each measure column you identify on the left axis is represented as a line of a different color.

You are required to designate at least one column on the left axis. The bottom axis and legend elements are optional, but at least one is needed to display anything meaningful in your line chart.

Some Other Visual Views
There are two additional views that I want to describe in this section. Though they are not considered Chart views in Answers On Demand, I consider them to be advanced charts or visual types of Report views. The configuration of these advanced charts is only slightly different from the configuration of the chart types within the Chart view.

Gauge   The Gauge view is an impressive visual element that you can add to your reports. The clarity of the data is not necessarily enhanced, but the visual interest of your report may be enhanced greatly. This type of view on a real-time report showing data that changes often can be fun to watch and informative as the user refreshes the report.

To add gauges to your report, click the Add View button on the Step 2 screen and select Gauge. The Edit View screen for the Gauge view is quite similar to the Edit View screen you use for charts. The buttons in the header are different and are specific to the Gauge view.

The first button on the title bar is the Gauge Canvas Properties button. The icon is the same as the General Chart Properties button in the Edit view for charts. Click this button and the Gauge Canvas Properties window opens.

On the Gauge Canvas Properties window, you can format the title, legend location, borders and colors, and the gauge layout. By default, your Gauge view title will reflect the name of the measure displayed on the gauges. To change the title, click the Custom Title check box and type your desired title in the Title field. Click the Text Format button next to the Title field to set the font family, color, style, and font size for your title on the Text Format window.

The Legend Location field provides some control over if and where your gauge legend appears. You can choose to display your legend on the top (default), left, right, or bottom of your chart. You may also select None to remove the legend from your chart. The format button next to the Location field provides some typical text-formatting controls.

In the Borders & Colors section of the Gauge Canvas Properties window, there is a Color Selector for the background and the text. The text color does not appear to affect the text on a Gauge view, but the background color is effective and really highlights the gauges on the canvas, as the background color affects all of the background except for the circular area around each gauge. You will also see a border Color selector here, but the check box to disable the border is read-only. If you want to eliminate your border, simply use the border Color Selector to set the border color to the same color as your background.

Gauge Layout, the final section of this window, contains two fields for adjusting the number of gauges that appear in each row on the gauge canvas and the amount of space between the gauges. Experiment with adding values to these two fields. The space between gauges is measured in points and affects both horizontal and vertical spacing.

The next button on the title bar is the Gauge Titles button. This button opens the Gauge Titles window, which contains four fields and text-formatting buttons. Each gauge can have a title and subtitle above the gauge and a footer and secondary footer below the gauge. Text that you type into any of these fields will appear on every gauge in the canvas. You may also reference columns in the report using a bit of shorthand, where @1 is the first column in the report, @2 is the second, and so on. Using the column reference in the title fields gives you the value from that column on the gauge associated with each row of data. Format each title's appearance using the text format button next to the Title field.

The next button is the Gauge Ranges button. This button takes you to the Gauge Ranges window, where you are able to identify the size and number of segments that your gauge scales display. The default is a scale of 0 to 100 percent split into three even segments. You can manually change the minimum and maximum value ranges for each section. You may also change the caption of the sections by typing a new caption into the Caption field. This caption appears in the legend on the gauge canvas. Click the Color Selector to change the default color for the gauge segments.

If you want more than three segments on your gauges, click the Add button to insert an additional segment. One really convenient feature here is that by leaving the minimum and maximum values fields blank, the gauge will automatically divide into even sections with the specified number of segments. Removing a segment is as simple as clicking the X button to the right of the segment.

To the right of the Gauge Ranges button is the Additional Gauge Properties button. This, of course, opens the Additional Gauge Properties window, which contains three tabs, each dedicated to a different element of your chart. The first tab is the Appearance tab. Here you can specify if and when data labels appear on your gauges and their format. In the Borders & Colors section, you can set the background color and text color for your gauges. The background color in this case is the background of the gauge itself, not the canvas. The text color option is misleading. The color you select here affects only the tick marks on the gauge. Click the Show Border check box to add a border that encircles each gauge. Once activated, you are able to use the Color Selector to specify a color for your border.

In the Size section, you are able to customize the width and height of your gauges. Since the gauges are circular, specifying either a height or width will change the size of the gauge evenly. If you enter different numbers in the Width and Height fields, your gauges will stretch into an oval shape rather than maintain their circular shape.

The next tab, Scale, allows you to set the upper and lower limits of your gauge scale. The Advanced Options button next to the Minimum and Maximum fields opens the Advanced Options window allowing you to identify a column to set your gauge limit on. Also on this tab, you can change the number of major or minor tick marks. These are the marks around the inside of your dial gauge. In the Labels section, you can format the scale labels by selecting a font family, color, text style, and font size.

The Interaction tab allows you to select the type of interaction that will occur when a user clicks the gauge. The default setting is Drill. You may disable interactivity or set up a navigation path to another report.

The final button, in the shape of a star, is the Advanced Properties button. This button opens a properties window specific to the gauge type selected in the Gauge field to the right of the button. Within the Gauge field, you will notice that you can select Dial, Bar, or Bulb. The Advanced Properties button is available for the dial and bar gauge types.

With the dial gauge, the Dial Specific Properties window opens when you click the Advanced Properties button. Here you are able to specify how the scale labels should appear inside the dial. Your options are to show percentage of total (default) or the actual measure values. You can also choose to not display scale labels. You are also able to adjust the arc length of your dial gauge and the thickness. The dial arc length is measured in degrees, so the valid range of values in this field is 0 to 360. Enter a thickness in points if you want to thicken your dial.

If you are working with bar gauges, which I describe next, this Advanced Properties button opens the Bar-Specific Properties window with two check boxes. Your options here are to enable or disable the color bar and scale below the bar gauges.

To the right of the buttons in the title bar, you have three fields. The Gauge field allows you to select one of three gauge styles. The dial gauge is the default, but you also have the option of using a bar gauge or a bulb gauge. The bar gauge fills from left to right according to the measure for the gauge. The bulb gauge simply changes color according to the measure for the gauge. The bar and bulb gauges permit only one measure.

The Type field, which is available only with the bar and bulb gauges, allows you to select the fill type (default) or the LED type for the bar gauge. The Type field for the bulb gauge gives you the option of a two-dimensional or three-dimensional appearance for your gauges.

Finally, the Size field gives you the option of small, medium (default), large, or custom-size gauges. If you select Custom in the Type field, the Additional Gauge Properties window opens where you may set the size of the gauges. You are able to make additional special formatting changes by clicking the Advanced Properties button. The small-size gauge is preset to an 80-point width. Medium is 150 points wide, and large is 200 points wide.

The area to the left of the gauge canvas preview identifies the current measure columns for your Gauge view. The dial gauges permit more than one measure column on each gauge. With the dial gauges, you may select the measure column using the Measure field. In the Marker Type field you are able to select the compass (default), arrow, or line marker types. This setting changes the pointer in the dial. The Color Selector allows you to set a specific color for each measure column. The Marker Type and Color fields are disabled for the bar and bulb gauges. To add a marker to your dial gauge, click the Add Marker button and set the measure, marker type, and color attributes for the new marker. Remove markers by clicking the X button next to the measure column you wish to remove.

Funnel Chart   The final visual view I want to describe here is the funnel chart. Funnel charts are most popular among the sales departments of the corporate world, as they provide an interesting view of how sales deals at different stages are performing against goals. Funnel charts have rather limited applicability, and require a specific type of data to be meaningful, but when placed in the right type of report can be highly informative.

To add a funnel chart to your report, click the Add View button, move to the Advanced submenu, and select Funnel Chart. The Edit View screen for the funnel chart is relatively simple without an abundance of formatting options.

To add a title to your funnel chart, enter it in the Chart Title field. Notice that the format text button is not present here, as it is with other text fields. Three columns are required to build a funnel chart. The Stage element defines the segments of the funnel. Actual Value and Target Value identify the metric columns that are compared within the funnel. The funnel chart will fill and color each portion of the funnel according to the relationship between these two values and the threshold percentages. Any segment of the funnel where the percentage of the target value represented by the actual value is less than the minimum threshold percentage appears in red on the funnel. If this calculation falls between the minimum and maximum threshold percentages, the segment is colored yellow. Values above the maximum threshold appear green on the funnel. You can adjust these thresholds in the Minimum Threshold and Maximum Threshold fields.

Your funnel chart can reflect the number of records in each stage by making the segments wider for more records and narrower for a smaller number of records. If you want your chart to look more like a funnel, click the Force Standard Shape And Equal Stage Widths check box. The chart will show each segment with the same width, so you lose the perception of size of each stage segment, but your chart looks a bit neater.

The Size field allows you to scale the entire chart with sizes between 10 and 100 in increments of 10. Again, your ability to customize this chart is quite limited compared to others. Notice there is no way to adjust the text, colors, borders, or backgrounds.

For certain data sets you may want to only identify your target value in the final stage. Click the Target Value For Final Stage Only check box. This makes the Factor Required To Meet Target field available for editing. I recommend using these options only if you already understand the advanced accounting concepts that go into factoring data in the funnel.

Pivot Tables

Pivot tables are, by far, the most flexible, most configurable, most complex, and most commonly used view on all types of reports. Unlike a normal Table view, the Pivot Table view allows you to move data around, organize metrics into columns, create sections of data by segment, and create separate pages for data based on a particular column value. Pivot tables can take on many different forms and serve a multitude of purposes.

A Pivot Table view is made up of six different layout areas into which you can place your data columns. Each area serves a specific purpose and has a different set of formatting options. Your data columns make up the data layer. You can also apply some special formatting to this layer. The most basic pivot table is a simple reorganization of report data into the pivot table layout areas.

Each area in the pivot table layout serves a different purpose and has different effects on the data that appears in your pivot table. As you move columns in and out of these areas, the preview below will refresh to show the new arrangement.

The Rows area organizes data into rows, grouping the data from left to right, very much like a normal Table view. You can change this horizontal grouping by changing the order of the columns in the Rows area.

The Measures area typically contains metric columns. This area is where any measures associated with the values in the Rows and Columns areas are displayed. You may also place nonmetric data in the Measures area. You will notice that the column values appear null when in the Measures area. This is because nonmetric columns have a default aggregation rule of "none."

Create a cross-tab matrix by adding database columns to the Columns area. Your pivot table will have a column for each value in the database column. The values in the Measures area will now relate to both the rows and columns where each row intersects each column. The combination of the Rows, Measures, and Columns areas is considered the content portion of the pivot table.

Placing a column in the Sections area in your pivot table will separate the pivot table content into a separate table for each value in the section area column. For instance, placing the User Name column in the Sections area creates a separate table for each user.

Placing a column in the Pages area has a similar effect as the Sections area, only the Pivot Table view will show only one table at a time based on the column value selected from a drop-down list above the table. Each value in the column is a value in the drop-down list, and selecting a new value in this field changes the pivot table below to show only data related to the selected value.

The excluded area is a place to put any columns that you do not want affecting your pivot table. Any columns placed in this area are removed from the Pivot Table view, but not the report. The ability to exclude columns makes it possible to include multiple Pivot Table views with different content in your report.

The Pivot Table view is rather useful, even without a lot of formatting. The ability to rearrange the data and show multiple views of the same data is a great asset to your reporting design, but that is only the beginning. With some basic formatting and even a little creative formatting, the Pivot Table view can take on appearances well beyond the basics.

View Properties

Most of the formatting of pivot tables takes place within the pivot table areas and on the columns themselves. There is a single property affecting the entire pivot table that you are able to modify. In the title bar on the Edit View screen for your pivot table you will find the Pivot Table View Properties button. Clicking this button opens the Edit View window. The only property you can edit here is the "green bar" styling. Clicking the check box enables this styling and causes every other row in the pivot table to take on a light green background. The Alternate field lets you choose to shade every other row, beginning with the innermost column, or to alternate the rows across the entire table. The innermost column is the last column in the Rows area of your pivot table. The rows in the Measures area are given the alternating style when you set the alternate method to either Innermost Column or All Columns.

You do not have to accept the default format of the "green bar" styling. You can make the alternating rows any color you please by clicking the Set Alternate Format button. This button opens the standard Edit Format window, allowing you to set the format for the font, cell, and border of every other row.

Adding Totals and Formatting the Rows Area

In the Rows area, to the right of the word "Rows" in the upper left, you see a Totals (Σ) button. The letter sigma is a mathematical symbol for sum. Click this button to open the Total menu. Initially, the None option is selected, indicating that no totals are included in the pivot table for the rows. To add totals, select either the Before or After option. The Before option creates a Grand Total row at the top of your pivot table, and the After option gives you a Grand Total row at the bottom of your pivot table. The total of the metric columns appears and aggregates the data across all rows based on the aggregation rule for the metric column. You can display this Grand Total row before or after the measure values, not both.

The default label for the row total is "Grand Total." You can change this if you like, along with the format of the label, by again clicking the Σ button and selecting Format Labels. A typical Edit Format window opens, but with the addition of a Folder field at the top of the window. The Folder field, despite the misleading name, is actually tied to the label for the row total. Enter a new label into this field. You may also apply any formatting options to the font, cell, or border as you normally would.

You can also format the values in the total row by clicking the Σ button and selecting Format Values. Again, a typical Edit Format window opens where you can format the font, cell, and border for the measure values in the total row.

Adding Totals and Formatting the Columns Area

You may have noticed that your Columns area contains a Measure Labels object. The Measure Labels object contains two buttons. The first is a More Options button and the second is a Totals button. You will also notice that you have a Totals button to the right of the word "Columns" in the upper-left corner of the Columns area, just like the one in the Rows area. These two Totals buttons are redundant, except that the Totals button on the Measure Labels object is fully functional while the other will insert a total column, but its formatting options are not functional.

For this reason, I recommend we ignore the Σ button on the Columns area and use only the buttons on the Measure Labels object to insert and format totals in the Columns area.

Click the Σ button to open the Total menu on the Measure Labels object in the Columns area. The default option of None is initially selected here, too. To add a total column, select the Before, After, At The Beginning, or At The End option. The total column will contain a total of each metric across all columns in each row.

Column totals are really only applicable when you have split a metric into multiple columns by adding a database column to the Columns area and want to see a total across all of those columns. If you do not want to intermingle these individual total columns within the metric columns, you can choose to group all of your total columns together.

Click the Σ button to open the Total menu on the Measure Labels object in the Columns area. The At The Beginning option creates a set of total columns before all of the individual metric columns.

The default label on your total columns consists of the column name being totaled followed by "Total." You can change this if you like, along with the format of the label, by again clicking the Σ button and selecting Format Labels. A typical Edit Format window opens, but with the addition of a Folder field at the top of the window. Just like changing the label on the Grand Total row, enter a new label into the Folder field. The text you type into the Folder field is applied to all of your total columns, which could become confusing if you have multiple metrics in your pivot table, so you will probably want to keep the name of the metric in the total column. You can do this by entering the at sign (@) into your new label.

The other formatting options for the label affect only the labels for the total columns. If you want to modify the measure labels (the column name, not the value name) of the metric columns, you can click the More Options button. This opens another menu. Select Format Measure Labels to open an Edit Format window that allows you to format all of the measure labels. If you have not already formatted the total column labels, the measure labels format will also format the labels on the total columns.

The More Options menu also includes an option to hide the measure labels. Select Hidden, and the labels showing the name of the columns in the Measures area are hidden from sight in the pivot table. This option does not hide the labels on any total columns that you have added in the Columns area.

You can also format the values in the total columns by clicking the Σ button and selecting Format Values. Again, a typical Edit Format window opens where you can format the font, cell, and border for the measure values in the total columns.

Adding Totals and Formatting the Sections Area

As you know, the Sections area allows you to split your pivot table into separate tables—one for each value in a column. Well, what if you want to have the entire pivot table for all values and the individual tables? To the right of the word "Sections" in the upper left, you see yet another Σ button. Click this button, and you see a familiar menu. Adding a total on the Sections area adds a pivot table to the view. This additional table is a summary of all sections. You can place this summary table before the other sections by selecting the Before option or after the other sections by selecting the After option on the Section Totals menu.

The default label on this summary table is "All Sections." You can change by selecting the Format Labels option in the Section Total menu. The Folder field allows you to add your own label to the total table. The other format settings on the Edit Format window apply to this label as well. The Format Values option on the Section Totals menu affects the values within the measures of your section summary table.

The second button in the Sections area is the Section Properties button. Clicking this button opens the Section Properties window where you are able to configure the display of column headings on the columns in your Section area. You will also find options for inserting a page break and showing blank rows.

You have four options for displaying the column headings within your section. The column heading, by default, is not displayed, showing only the column value in the Sections area. If you want to display the column headings in the Sections area, click the option next to the location of your choice. You can select Above, Left, or Before. Left and Before are similar. Left places the column heading to the left of the column value, but treats the heading and the value as if they are in separate cells. If you are displaying multiple rows of values in the section, the headings and values will align across the rows. The Before option places the heading to the left of the value, separated by a space, as if concatenated into a single value.

In the Options section of the Section Properties window the Insert Page Break field provides you with the ability to insert a page break between sections. Your page breaks are only in effect when you print the report to a PDF file. The Insert Page Break field will have at least four options, but will have more if you add more than one column to the Sections area.

Of course, No Page Break is the default setting. The next two values are Innermost Column and Outermost Column. The innermost column is the last column in the Sections area. The page break function inserts a page break after every unique section based on the column selected in this field. Uniqueness of sections is based on the section column values from the outermost column to the innermost column. Selecting Innermost Column in this field will guarantee that each section is on its own page.

You will also notice that each column present in your Sections area appears in the list of values for the Insert Page Break field. If you have more than two columns in your Sections area, you will have more than just an innermost column and outermost column to choose from. You can insert a page break after sections based on any column by selecting the column in this field. Remember that uniqueness is determined from the first column working inward, so selecting the second of three columns will group all sections where the first two section columns are the same onto the same page.

If you add a column to the Sections area that is blank on some of the records, you will have a section with no name. The Pivot Table view truncates out the space that would otherwise be occupied by a value. The difference is subtle, but clicking the Show Blank Rows check box causes the pivot table to retain this space.

The cell and border format options affect the section header area above the table in each section. The line that appears by default above the section name is a top border on the Sections area. If you want to change or remove this border, you will make that change here. The additional formatting options on the Section Properties window affect the text area of the section header and do not change the size of the section header.

Adding Totals and Formatting the Pages Area

When you add a column to the Pages area, a drop-down list appears at the top of your pivot table that works like a filter. This page filter field gives you the ability to dynamically change the content of the pivot table based on a selected value. The field contains only the values in the column. Suppose you want to also have the option of seeing all of the values in the one pivot table.

To the right of "Pages" in the upper left, you see Pages area's Σ button. Click this button, and you see a familiar menu. Adding a total on the Pages area adds the All Pages option to the drop-down list. Since the pivot table will display the first page in the list when the report initially runs, if you select Before in the Totals menu, your pivot table will default to show all pages when the report runs. Selecting After places the All Pages option at the end of the list. The All Pages option is only available for the first column in the Pages area.

Content Properties

You may have noticed that there is an area between the Sections area and Rows area and to the left of the Columns area. You are not able to drop a column into this area. The only object here is a Content Properties button. Content, in this case, is defined as the Rows, Columns, and Measures areas of the pivot table. Click this button and the Content Properties window opens.

At the top of this window you find three check boxes, the third of which is selected by default. The first option here is to hide the content of the pivot table. If you have not added any columns to your Pages or Sections area, your pivot table essentially disappears.

If you have added a column to your Columns area in your pivot table, you may have noticed that there are columns present that do not contain any data and are not needed in the pivot table. Another situation that leads to blank columns is a pivot table with the same column placed in both the Sections area and the Columns area, which is not unusual at all. The second check box on the Content Properties window serves to remedy this design issue. When you choose to limit columns based on section values, any column that has no values in it will not appear in the section's pivot table.

The third check box in the Content Properties window limits rows based on section values. This check box is selected by default, as it is unusual to want to show blank rows within your table.

The formatting options on the Content Properties screen affect the entire content area. Again, the content area is the Rows, Columns, and Measures areas. Here you may add a background color to the entire content area, add a border, and adjust the alignment of the entire table. By default, pivot tables center themselves. Often, it is more desirable to move the entire table to the left. You would make that adjustment here.

Formatting Columns in Your Pivot Table

On each database column that you have added to your Pivot Table view, you will find up to three buttons next to the column name. All of the columns have a More Options button. Many will have the Σ button. You will also find that columns in any area other than the Measures area have a sort button.

The availability of many of these buttons and the options beneath them are dependant on the area and, in some cases, the location within the area of the pivot table. There are, however, several options that are common across all columns.

Click the More Options button and select Format Headings from the menu. This opens the Edit Format window. To change the heading on the column, type a new value in the Folder field. The remaining options on the Edit Format screen also affect the heading for that column in your pivot table.

While the formatting affects only the heading on the column, if you adjust the width of the heading using the additional formatting options, the entire column, including the column values, adjusts according to the width setting. It is not possible to widen the heading and not the values. The inverse is also true, as formatting the value width also affects the heading. If you adjust both the column heading width and the column value width, the larger of the two settings will control the width of the column. Concerning text alignment within the heading and values area, the width setting does affect the location of the center or left side of the column.

Click More Options and select Format Values to open the Edit Format window for the values portion of the column. I often find myself needing to apply the same formatting across many column headings or column values in my pivot tables. After formatting one heading the way I like, I click the copy icon in the upper-right portion of the Edit Format screen, and then paste my formatting into the other column headings.

If you want to include one of your columns in your pivot table more than once, click the More Options button and select Duplicate Layer. This inserts an exact copy of the column into the same area. The copy will retain any formatting that you applied to the original column before creating the duplicate. You can now move this duplicate to any of the other areas and apply formatting.

Duplicating a column is often quite useful when you want to show a column value in a pivot table section and rows, for instance, or perhaps you want to include a measure in a pivot table twice with different aggregation rules.

Once you have added a duplicate, a new menu option becomes available on both the original and duplicate column. Click the More Options button and select Remove Duplicate to remove that copy of the column from the pivot table.

Click the More Options button and select Remove Column, and you will be removing the column from the entire report. This means that you are not only removing the column from the pivot table, but all other views too. If you select the Remove Column option, a confirmation dialog box appears confirming that this is what you really intend to do. Remember, if you want to remove a column from the pivot table only, drag it to the Excluded area.

In addition to the options in the More Options menu that are common to all columns added to a pivot table, every column outside of the Measures area has a sort button. To override default sorting in your pivot table, click the Sort button on the column you want to sort on. Sorting within the pivot table is quite different from sorting in a normal table.

Sorting only affects the area that contains the column. Sorting a column in the Pages area changes the order of the values in the page drop-down list. Sorting a column in the Sections area affects the order in which the sections appear in the Pivot Table view.

In the Rows area, the grouping effect restricts the sort of column values within the confines of the column to the left.

Formatting Columns in the Rows Area

A column's More Options menu changes based on the area of the pivot table to which the column is assigned. Columns in the Rows area have two additional options: Hidden and New Calculated Item.

Click the More Options button and select Hidden to hide a column in your pivot table. Just like hiding a column in a regular table, the column continues to affect the table, but does not appear in the results. If you simply excluded the column from the report, the values within that column would have no effect on your pivot table.

You can still sort on a hidden column, which is useful if you want to sort by a specific column but want the values displayed in a location that would sort incorrectly based on the grouping of data.

Within the areas of the pivot table, you are able to add totals for the columns within the area. These totals are grand totals of all values. On the specific columns, you are able to add subtotals for each column value. When you have two or more columns in the Rows area, all but the innermost column will have a Totals (Σ) button.

Click this button to open the Total menu. Initially, the None option is selected, indicating that no subtotals are included in the pivot table for the row. To add subtotals, select the Before, After, At The Beginning, or At The End option. The Before option creates a total over each value in the column. The After option gives you a total row after each value. The At The Beginning and At The End options will group all of your subtotal rows together at the top or bottom of the table, respectively.

If you want to display a row label between each value in a column but do not want to show the totals, select the Labels Only (No Totals) option in the Totals menu. A blank row bearing the name of the column value is inserted into the table based on the location checked above.

The default label for the row total shows the row value followed by the word "Total." You can change this if you like, along with the format of the label, by again clicking the Σ button and selecting Format Labels. A typical Edit Format window opens, but with the addition of a Folder field at the top of the window. Enter a new label into this field. You may also apply any formatting options to the font, cell, or border as you normally would.

If you want to retain the value name in the heading, you can use the "" wildcard to represent the value name. For instance, if you type **@ Subtotal** in the Folder field, your total row will display the value name followed by "Subtotal."

You can also format the values in the total row by clicking the Σ button and selecting Format Values. Again, a typical Edit Format window opens, where you can format the font, cell, and border for the measure values in the total row.

Formatting Columns in the Columns Area

Similar to the fields in the Rows area, in the Columns area, you gain the option for new calculated items and also the ability to add subtotals. The functionality is the same as described in the Rows area, but the location and purpose is somewhat different due to the location of the columns.

While describing the pivot table areas earlier, I mentioned adding totals on the Measure Labels object. There, we saw that you are able to insert a totals column for each measure column. The Totals button on the columns in the Columns area allows you to insert a total column for each value in a column when you have more than one column here. As you add columns, the order of the columns controls how the columns are displayed in the pivot table. The individual values for the second column are grouped beneath each value in the first column.

All columns in the Columns area except for the last column have a Totals (Σ) button. Click this button to open the Total menu. Initially, the None option is selected, indicating that no subtotal columns are included in the pivot table. To add subtotals, select the Before, After, At The Beginning, or At The End option. The Before option creates a total column before each value in the column. The After option gives you a total column after each value. The At The Beginning and At The End options will group all of your subtotal rows together at the top or bottom of the table, respectively.

The default label for the column total shows the column value followed by the word "Total." You can change this if you like, along with the format of the label, by again clicking the Σ button and selecting Format Labels. A typical Edit Format window opens, but with the addition of a Folder field at the top of the window. Enter a new label into this field. You may also apply any formatting options to the font, cell, or border as you normally would. Like before, if you want to retain the value name in the heading, you can use the "" wildcard to represent the value name.

You can also format the values in the total column by clicking the Σ button and selecting Format Values. Again, a typical Edit Format window opens, where you can format the font, cell, and border for the measure values in the total row.

Formatting Columns in the Measures Area

The More Options button on columns in the Measures area contains some very different options from the other areas. You can transform your measure values into percentages and indexes of portions of your data, change the way data aggregates, and display running totals. You could perform many of these calculations on the column directly on step 1 of the Build And View Analysis screen, but the formulae required to group the data and perform the calculations is a bit more complex.

Click the More Options button and move your mouse to the Show Data As option. Another submenu opens showing three options. By default, your measure columns are set to show the data values. You also see options here for Percent Of and Index Of.

Move your mouse over the Percent Of option and you will see another submenu with options for showing the values as a percentage of the column, row, section, page, column parent, row parent, or layer. Select one of these options to change the column values to a percentage calculation.

Select the Percent Of Column option to see the calculated percentage of the column represented by the value in each row. When you have not added any columns to the Columns area, the Percent Of Row option results in 100 percent for each row, as the value displayed in that row is 100 percent of that value in that row. When you are grouping data into column values, this option will give you the percentage that the column value represents within that row.

The Percent Of Section option converts the column values into a percentage of the section. The values in the columns will total to 100 percent for each section of the Pivot Table view. Likewise, the Percent Of Page option converts the column values into a percentage of the page represented by each value. All of the percentages in the entire Pivot Table view will total to 100 percent.

If you have multiple columns in the Columns area or multiple rows in the Rows area, you may find that you need to select the Percentage Of Column Parent or Percentage Of Row Parent option. This will give you the percentage of the topmost column or outermost row, respectively.

The Percent Of Layer option allows you select the exact column for which you want to see the percentage. This may be necessary when the desired column is not represented by the page, section, row parent, or column parent.

The Index Of option contains the same submenu options as the Percent Of option, and provides the exact same functionality in a different format. The Percent Of option results in values reflected as percentages. The Index

Of option results in index values. So if you would rather see ".38" than "38%," use the Index Of option.

You can use a different aggregation rule in the pivot table than you do on the column directly on step 1 of the Build And View Analysis screen. This allows you to duplicate columns and display different calculations for the same columns, for instance.

To set the aggregation rule on a measure column, click the More Options button and move your mouse to Aggregation Rule. A submenu displays, showing all of the available aggregation rules. Twelve values are available for your pivot table measure column value aggregation.

If you want to display your column values as a running sum across the rows of data, click the More Options button and select the Display A Running Sum option. The aggregation rule on the column affects this calculation too. An aggregation rule of Count coupled with the Display As Running Sum option results in a running count in the column.

Formatting Columns in the Sections Area

Columns that you add to the Sections area control the way that the pivot table breaks into smaller tables within the Pivot Table view. In the More Options menu of columns in the Sections area you will find some of the same options I described in other areas in addition to a couple of new options we have not yet discussed.

The Hidden option hides the column values, just like in other areas, but when the column is in the Sections area, the application of the effect is a little different. Since each section contains a separate table based on the columns in the Sections area, hiding the column here causes the value to disappear but retains the splits based on the values in the column. This potentially results in an unlabeled section.

You may have a good reason for hiding a column value here if you want to split the table based on some criteria but do not want to display that value and instead display the values in another column that you have included in the Sections area.

When you add multiple columns to the Sections area, it is the combination of these columns that determines what the section contains. Each unique combination of column values from each column results in a separate section. The column values are initially displayed on a single line separated only by a space. If you are displaying column headings in your sections, the headings and values are all strung together in a single line.

To show each value on a separate line in the section heading, click the More Options button on a column you want to move to the next line, and select the Place Value In New Row option. The column value, and heading if displayed, moves to the next line in the section heading.

When you have multiple columns in your Sections area, you will find that the first column value is repeated for each of the values in the second column. You may want to display the value from the first column in the first section, but then only show the value from the second column in the remaining sections until the next value in the first column is reached. To accomplish this effect, click the More Options button on the first column and select the Hide Repeated Values option.

Just as we are able to add column totals in the Rows and Columns areas, the Totals button on the columns in the Sections area allows you to insert a summary section for each value in a column. You will need more than one column in the Sections area to have this option available. As you add columns, the order of the columns controls how the sections are created and ordered in the pivot table. The individual values for the second column are combined with each value in the first column to form unique sections.

All columns in the Sections area, except for the last column, have a Totals (Σ) button. Click this button to open the Total menu. Initially, the None option is selected, indicating that no summary sections are included in the pivot table. To add a summary section, select the Before, After, At The Beginning, or At The End option. The Before option creates a total section before each section containing a unique value in the column. The After option gives you a total section after the sections for each value in that column. The At The Beginning and At The End options will group all of your total sections before or after all of the sections, respectively.

The default label for the summary section shows the column value followed by the word "Total." You can change this if you like, along with the format of the label, by again clicking the Σ button and selecting Format Labels. A typical Edit Format window opens, but with the addition of a Folder field at the top of the window. Enter a new label into this field. You may also apply any formatting options to the font, cell, or border as you normally would. Like before, if you want to retain the value name in the heading, you can use the "" wildcard to represent the value name.

You can also format the values in the summary section by clicking the Σ button and selecting Format Values. Again, a typical Edit Format window opens where you can format the font, cell, and border for the measure values in the section.

Formatting Columns in the Pages Area

Columns that you add to the Pages area control the content of the Page Selector drop-down list. This area uses column values in a very different way than the other areas, so it stands to reason that the options on the columns here are a little different too. In the More Options menu of columns in the Pages area you will find some of the same options but the effects are unique.

The Hidden option hides the column values just like in other areas, but since the column values in the Pages area are displayed as values in a drop-down list, the application of the effect is rather counterproductive. Since the combination of column values determines the content of the Page Selector, hiding one of the columns causes repeating values in the drop-down list. I have never needed to do this.

If you are creating a separate drop-down list for each column, hiding a column results in an error, as you must display at least one value per drop-down list.

When you add multiple columns to the Pages area, it is the combination of these columns that determines what the pivot table page contains. Each unique combination of column values from each column results in a separate page. The column headings are initially displayed on a single line separated by a hyphen, and the values on the single drop-down list are also displayed hyphenated.

To create a new drop-down list for each column, click the More Options button on the column and select the Start New Page Dropdown option. A new drop-down list for the column appears on the next line in the Pages area of the pivot table.

As with the other areas, you will find the New Calculated Item option on your More Options menu for the columns in the Pages area. The New Calculated Item gives us the same flexibility here as in the other areas, only the values appear in the drop-down lists. You can use calculated items in the Pages area to filter out pages or to group data into single pages. The process for creating a new calculated item here is the same as in other areas of the pivot table.

Just as we are able to add column totals to create a summary section in the Sections area, you can also create summary page options in the Page Selector drop-down list. All columns in the Pages area, except for the last column, have a Totals (Σ) button. Click this button to open the Total menu. Initially, the None option is selected. To add a summary page, select the Before, After, At The Beginning, or At The End option. The Before option creates a page value in the list before each column value. The After option gives you the additional page value after each column value in the drop-down list. The At The Beginning and At The End options will group all of your total pages before or after all of the values in the drop-down list, respectively.

The default label for the new value is the column value followed by the word "Total." You can change this if you like by clicking the Σ button and selecting Format Labels. A typical Edit Format window opens with the Folder field at the top of the window. Enter a new label into this field. Like before, if you want to retain the value name in the heading, you can use the "" wildcard to represent the value name.

Since the label for the new page actually appears in the drop-down list, any format changes you make beyond the name are ignored. You can format the values in the summary pages by clicking the Σ button and selecting Format Values. Again, a typical Edit Format window opens, where you can format the font, cell, and border for the measure values in the section. When you display a summary page in the report, the data is formatted according to the settings here.

Pivot Charts

On the Edit View screen for the Pivot Chart view, you will find a Chart Pivoted Results check box and Chart Position field in the header bar. Click this check box, and a chart based on your pivot chart data is inserted into the Pivot Chart view at the location selected in the Chart Position field. Most of the basic charts are available as a pivot chart, but there are some differences in how you format the charts. Bubble charts and scatter charts are not available as pivot charts.

Pivot charts are based on the rows, columns, and measures in your pivot table. To insert a chart, click the Chart Pivoted Results check box. The default position is to the right of the pivot table, but you can choose to place the pivot chart on the left, top, or bottom. You can also hide the pivot table and display only the charted pivot data.

One thing you will notice about pivot charts is that you do not select the columns you want to display and assign the axis on which column data displays. The control for this is in the layout of your pivot table. The location of the row data, column data, and measures differs by chart. Notice the differences between Figures 2-19 and 2-20. Both pivot tables and charts

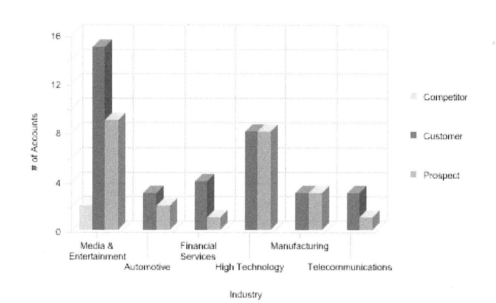

Industry	# of Accounts		
	Competitor	Customer	Prospect
Media & Entertainment	2	15	9
Automotive		3	2
Financial Services		4	1
High Technology		8	8
Manufacturing		3	3
Telecommunications		3	1

Refresh - Printer Friendly - Download

FIGURE 2-19. *Pivot Chart – Industry rows by account type columns*

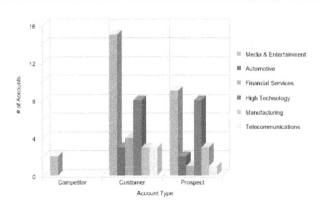

Account Type	# of Accounts					
	Media & Entertainment	Automotive	Financial Services	High Technology	Manufacturing	Telecommunications
Competitor	2					
Customer	15	3	4	8	3	3
Prospect	9	2	1	8	3	1

Refresh - Printer Friendly - Download

FIGURE 2-20. *Pivot Chart – Account type rows by industry columns*

provide the same data, but the arrangements of the values in the table and charts are different based on the placement of the row and column elements within the pivot table.

Select the graph, type, and style for your pivot chart, just like you would for a Chart view. Most of the chart controls for pivot charts are also the same as the controls available in the Chart view.

The first button in the toolbar is the General Chart Properties button. Click this button to add a title to your pivot chart, specify how labels will appear, change the data format, and specify the size for the chart. The only tangible difference between the Pivot Chart and a normal Chart view here has to do with the sizing of the chart. There are no slider bars for adjusting chart size like on the Chart view. To adjust Pivot Chart size, you enter the height and width here on the General Chart Properties window.

The next button is the Axis Titles And Labels button. Clicking this button opens the Axis Titles & Labels screen, which contains two or three tabs, depending on the chart type. The Left tab (and Right tab for a line bar combo chart) allows you to configure the title and label formats of the vertical axis. The Bottom tab also has a Title section and Labels section for modifying the title and scale labels of the bottom axis, respectively.

The next button is the Axis Scaling button. Clicking this button takes you to the Axis Scaling window. Your Axis Scaling window will have one or two tabs, depending on the type of chart. A line bar combo chart, for instance, has a scale on the left vertical axis and on the right vertical axis. Both the left and the right tabs on the Axis Scaling window contain the same fields, but may have different settings within those fields.

Here you can adjust the range of your axis scale and the number of major and minor tick marks. You can also add scale markers to your pivot charts.

To the right of the Axis Scaling button is the Additional Charting Options button. Clicking this opens the Additional Charting Options window. This window contains the Grid Lines tab, Legend tab, Interaction tab, and Borders & Colors tab.

On the Grid Lines tab you can change the color of the major and minor grid lines. Clicking the Override Defaults check box enables the check boxes on the tab that allow you to disable major, minor, vertical, and horizontal grid lines. On the Legend tab, you configure if and where your chart legend appears. The Interaction tab allows you to select the type of interaction that will occur when a user clicks part of the chart. The Borders & Colors tab allows you to set a color for your chart's background, text, and border.

The Format Chart Data button opens the Format Chart Data window, where you can format the appearance of your chart data elements. On a pivot chart, the Format Chart Data window contains two tabs. The Positional tab you are familiar with from the normal Chart view. On the Positional tab you can specify the color and style for each series and each chart component.

The Conditional tab gives you a formatting option that you do not have with the normal Chart view. On the Conditional tab, you will find each of the columns in your pivot chart listed on the left side of the tab.

Click the Add Condition button. A submenu appears that contains the list of columns in the pivot chart. Select the column to which you would like to add a conditional color format. A typical Create/Edit Filter window opens. Designate the operator and values for the condition and click OK. A new condition is added to the tab for the selected column. Click the Color box for the condition, and select a color from the palette. Now, whenever the condition is met, the chart element representing that column will change to the specified color.

You can continue to add conditions to the column, change their order using the arrow buttons, delete them using the X button, and modify the condition by clicking the Filter button.

With the line bar combo and pie charts, you are able to make additional special formatting changes by clicking the Advanced Properties button. On the line bar combo, the Chart Type Special window contains a single check box that allows you to synchronize the line and bar axis scales. For the pie chart, you are able to format the data values as a percentage of the total or the actual value represented by each wedge. You can also define what information is included in the data label. You can display the value only, the name only, or both name and value.

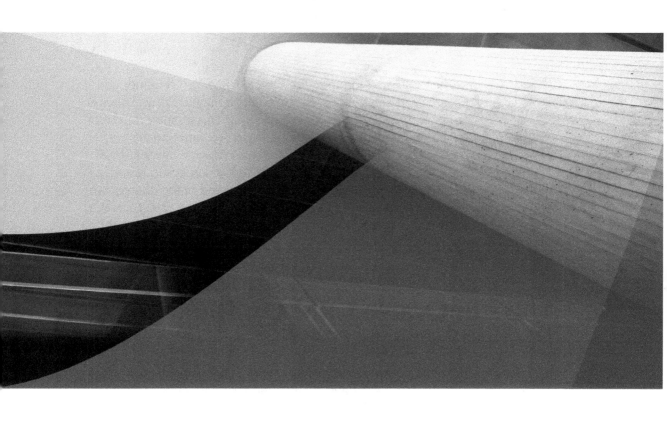

CHAPTER
3

Linking Reports

hen you are working with Oracle CRM On Demand, you are working with a website. No other feature of websites is more prevalent than then hyperlink. This chapter describes all of the methods for adding hyperlink functionality to Oracle CRM On Demand and your reports. We will look at linking between two reports, linking from non-report screens to reports, and linking from reports to non-report screens. At the end of the chapter we will try some other links that do not fit neatly into those three categories but that are potentially useful to you, the report developer, as you seek to add interactivity to your reports and further embed them into the business processes of your users.

URLs in Oracle CRM On Demand

I would be surprised if you were not already acquainted with the concept of a web address or URL (Uniform Resource Locator). Saying things like "www.oracle.com" in a normal conversation is as commonplace as a street address or phone number these days. New dictionaries are even including the word "dotcom" as part of English and other languages.

In order to be successful with embedding links to and from your reports in Oracle CRM On Demand, you will need to become familiar with the way these URLs work. The more you know about their structure, the way they are encoded, and their components, the more successful you will be. URLs require the same level of precision as coding in other computer languages. In fact, it is safe to presume that the URL language is just another programming language in that it has its own set of special characters and rules that must be followed in order for them to work.

Clearly, most URLs that you encounter are rather simple. A typical web address is nothing more than a string of common letters and dots. When you type www.oracle.com into your web browser's address field, you have entered a perfectly valid and extremely simple URL. Some assumptions are made for you, however. Your browser assumes that you really want to access http://www.oracle.com/index.html and fills in the blanks for you. In fact, in most browsers, you can type oracle.com and access the same site. You cannot rely on these assumptions when embedding links into Oracle CRM On Demand, however, so we will examine the URL in a bit more detail.

The structure of the URL is

```
<protocol:>//<host>/<url-path>
```

where the brackets separate the components and are not part of the actual URL. There are no spaces allowed in a URL. The URL http://www.oracle.com/index.html contains the protocol of http: and is followed by the two forward slashes. The host is www.oracle.com. The host identifies the computer where the information we want to access resides, and typically contains three parts. The first part references a specific computer, but is usually "www" for "World Wide Web." The second part identifies the local network where the computer resides. The third part is the top-level domain, which is intended to be descriptive of the type of site. So the host portion of this URL indicates that we want to access the oracle network (.oracle) on the World Wide Web (www), which is a commercial entity (.com).

Next in the URL is the URL path. This is the path (or directory location) to the particular page we want to download to our browser screen. The path is similar to the directory structure on your own computer, with the biggest difference being the use of forward slashes (/) rather than back slashes (\).

So far we have used a simple URL to examine the URL structure, but the report URLs you will encounter in CRM On Demand are not going to be so simple. Generally, URLs for reports are called Go URLs. A typical report Go URL looks something like this:

```
https://secure-ausomxdsa.crmondemand.com/OnDemand/user/analytics/
saw.dll?Go&Path=%2fshared%2fCompany_ML1234-1SML2_Shared_
Folder%2fMiscellaneous+Reports%2fSR+Escalation+Analysis&Options=
rfd&Action=Navigate&p0=1&p1=eq&p2=
%22Service+Request%22.%22Service+Request+ID%22&p3=%%%Id%%%
```

Table 3-1 breaks down this URL into its component parts. Many of the elements illustrated by this particular URL may be new to you, but are explained throughout this chapter. It is important that you recognize that this URL has no breaks or spaces. This is not always clear on the printed page due to line breaks.

Not all of the methods for linking to reports require the use of a specific URL, but for any that do, it is important that you ensure that your URL is encoded properly. Certain characters and spaces will break your URL. These characters may be included in your URL only if they are encoded. URL encoding involves replacing these unsafe characters with a three-

Component	Description
https://	This is the protocol. Note that the *s* in https:// indicates that you are connecting to a secure server.
secure-ausomxdsa .crmondemand.com	This is the host server you are connecting to. You may have been told at some point that your CRM On Demand application is hosted on a specific "pod." The pod is indicated by the three letters after "secure-ausomx" in the host name. The pod in this example is DSA.
/OnDemand/user/ analytics/saw.dll?Go	This is the Go path. This portion of the URL indicates that you are accessing the saw.dll and executing the Go command. The Go command accepts a range of tags that identify the report and how the report is accessed via the URL.
&Path=%2fshared% 2fCompany_ML1234- 1SML2_Shared_ Folder%2fMiscellaneo us+Reports%2fSR+Esc alation+Analysis	This is the Report path. The **&Path=** tag tells the Go Path which report to access. This path contains quite a lot of information. The folder structure includes the company identifier that points to the shared folder for your specific company. Remember, most customers are in a multitenant environment, so the pod you are accessing hosts many other companies. You will also notice the use of URL-encoded characters. Some characters, such as spaces and quotes and slashes, will break the URL if included in a URL string.
&Options=rfd	This is the **&Options=** tag, which controls which links appear at the bottom of the report when downloaded to your browser screen. As presented here, the standard Refresh, Printer Friendly, and Download links will be available for the report. Another option available here is the Modify Criteria link. This option can be included by adding *m* to the Options tag.

TABLE 3-1. *Sample Report URL Breakdown*

Component	Description
&Action=Navigate	This is the **&Action=** tag. This tag tells the application what to do with the report you are accessing. The Navigate value indicates that you are going to navigate to the report view. With this action you have the option of passing additional information to the report to filter the content. Other options here include Prompt, Print, and Download. Prompt is the default action and allows for any column filter prompts prior to taking you to the report. The Print and Download options will be described in detail a bit later in this chapter.
&p0=1&p1=eq&p2= %22Service+Request %22.%22Service+ Request+ID%22&p3= %%%Id%%%	The tags in this portion of the URL identify the number of filters applied, along with the filter operator, the column, and value for each filter. In this example, &p0=1 indicates that we are filtering one column. &p1=eq indicates that the filter condition is equals. &p2= %22Service+Request%22.%22Service+Request+ ID%22 indicates that we are filtering the "Service Request"."Service Request ID" column. Notice that the quotes and spaces are encoded. Finally, &p3= %%%Id%%% pulls the value of the ID column from the current service request record. This URL would be used in a Web Link to access a report filtering the report to the specific record from which it is linked. Tags can be added to filter additional columns.

TABLE 3-1. *Sample Report URL Breakdown* (continued)

character string that the browser translates into the proper character when executing the URL. Table 3-2 shows how the common unsafe characters should be encoded in your URLs.

Knowing the structure of the URL is extremely helpful when embedding links to your reports in Oracle CRM On Demand. Knowing how to find the URL for a specific report is much easier than trying to construct the URL

Character	Character URL Encoding	Character	Character URL Encoding
Space	%20 or +	;	%3b
!	%21	<	%3c
"	%22	=	%3d
#	%23	>	%3e
$	%24	?	%3f
%	%25	@	%40
&	%26	[	%5b
'	%27	\	%5c
(	%28	]	%5d
)	%29	^	%5e
*	%2a	_	%5f
+	%2b	`	%60
,	%2c	{	%7b
-	%2d	|	%7c
.	%2e	}	%7d
/	%2f	~	%7e
:	%3a		

TABLE 3-2. *URL Encoding*

entirely on your own. Each report has its own unique URL, and the best way to find that URL is to run your report from the Reports tab in Oracle CRM On Demand. The process for locating the URL is different, depending on the browser you are using.

If you are working in Internet Explorer, run your report and right-click in the body of the report after it loads. On the right-click menu, select Properties. On the Properties window (Figure 3-1), highlight the URL contained in the Address (URL) field. This *may* be the URL for your report, but I find that I usually need to click OK here, navigate back to the Reports tab and run the report a second time, then repeat the process for opening the Properties window to get the correct URL to appear here. Ultimately, the URL you are looking for will end with the Action=Prompt tag. If the URL shown here ends with "go," you will need to run the report again to get the correct URL.

Exactly why Oracle CRM On Demand shows different URLs in the Properties window from one time to the next has to do with the way the page is constructed within the browser, but either URL will take you to the report. The URL ending with the Action tag, however, is the one that we can use to modify and add tags to the URL.

If you are using the Firefox browser, finding the URL is slightly different. You still start by running the report from the Reports tab. Right-click in the body of the report, and in the right-click menu, select This Frame – View Frame Info. On the Frame Info screen (Figure 3-2), the Address field contains the URL for the report. You may find that you need to return to the Reports tab and run the report a second time to get the URL that ends with the Action=Prompt tag.

FIGURE 3-1. *Properties window*

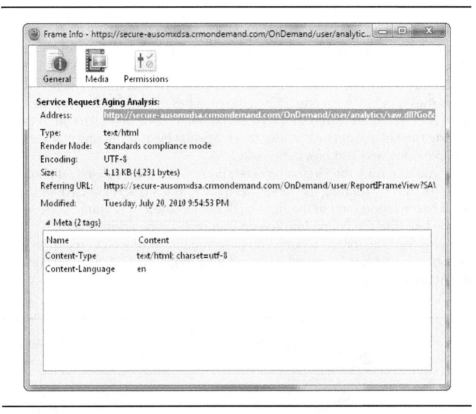

FIGURE 3-2. *Frame Info window*

Once you have found the correct URL for your report, copy it to your Clipboard so you can paste it into reports, Web Link fields, web applets, and other places as you link to and embed your report throughout Oracle CRM On Demand. I like to paste my URLs into a text editor and continue to modify them there before copying and pasting them back into Oracle CRM On Demand.

Go URL Tags

As you become familiar with the Go URL, you will find that it can do much more than just open a report. With a few modifications, the report URL that you use to link and embed your reports can save your users a lot of effort and ensure that your reports open and appear exactly the way you want them. The functionality of the URL is programmed using tags. These tags and their options are described in Table 3-3.

Tag	Values	Description
Path	Report Path	This is the report path. The path to the report is included in the default URL that you copy from the Properties or Frame Info window, as described previously. You will typically not change the contents of the Path tag when linking or embedding the report.
Options	r	The value of r provides the Refresh link at the bottom of the report.
	f	The value of f provides the Printer Friendly link at the bottom of the report.
	d	The value of d provides the download link at the bottom of the report.
	m	The value of m provides the Modify Criteria link at the bottom of the report.
		The Option tag can accept multiple values or no values. For example, Option=rfdm will result in all four links, while Option=fd will result in only the Printer Friendly and Download links. Option= with no values will result in no links at the bottom of the report.
Action	Prompt	Prompt is the default Action tag value. Prompt indicates that the report should open the column filter prompt if one exists on the report. Generally, when linking or embedding reports, it is not desirable to open column filter prompts. We normally change this value to Navigate for embedded reports.
	Navigate	The Navigate value bypasses any column filter prompts on the report and opens the report in the browser window. The Navigate action is most often used when linking or embedding a report and can be used in conjunction with the filter parameters described later to pass filter parameters to the report.

TABLE 3-3. *Go URL Tags*

Tag	Values	Description
	Print	The Print value works in conjunction with the Format tag and opens the report to the Printer Friendly view in the format identified in the Format tag. For instance, adding &Action=Print&Format=mht will open the report to the HTML printer friendly view.
		If your target report contains a table with multiple pages, the Print action will automatically expand the table to show all pages as long as you include a Format tag after the Action tag value.
		You cannot use multiple Action values, so if you need to pass filter values to your report, you will need to use the Navigate value and your users will need to click the Printer Friendly link to access the printer friendly view for the report—assuming you provide the link by also including the Options tag with the f value. The Options tag is not effective when using the Print Actions tag value.
	Download	The Download value works in conjunction with the Format tag and allows the user to download the report in the format identified in the Format tag. For instance, adding &Action=Download&Format=mht will open the File Download window, prompting the user to either open or save the .mht file.
		If your target report contains a table with multiple pages, the Download action will automatically expand the table to show all pages.
		If you neglect to include a Format tag in your URL, the CSV format will be used by default.
Format	pdf	Used in conjunction with the Print or Download Action tag values, the Format=pdf tag indicates that the report should be opened or downloaded in a PDF format.
	mht	Used in conjunction with the Print or Download Action tag values, the Format=mht tag indicates that the report should be opened or downloaded in an HTML format. This is the default format for the Print action if a Format tag is omitted.

TABLE 3-3. *Go URL Tags* (continued)

Tag	Values	Description
	excel	Used in conjunction with the Print or Download Action tag values, the Format=excel tag indicates that the report should be opened or downloaded in an Excel file format.
	csv	Used in conjunction with the Print or Download Action tag values, the Format=csv tag indicates that the report should be opened or downloaded in a comma-separated value format. This is the default format for the Download action if a Format tag is omitted. Charts are not included in the results when a report is formatted as a .csv document.
	txt	Used in conjunction with the Print or Download Action tag values, the Format=txt tag indicates that the report should be opened or downloaded in a plain-text file format. Charts are not included.
	xml	Used in conjunction with the Print or Download Action tag values, the Format=xml tag causes the report to open in an XML format. The XML for the report includes the report results, not the definition of the report.
P0	1-6	The P0 tag indicates the number of filters for which parameters will be passed to the report via the URL. The parameter tags that follow P0 work in sets of three to indicate the filter operator, filter column, and filter value. If filtering on a single column, you will set P0=1 and include P1, P2, and P3 tags to define the filter. If filtering on two columns, you will set P0=2 and include P1, P2, and P3 for the first filter and P4, P5, and P6 for the second filter. You can filter on up to six columns following this pattern.
P1 P4 P7 P10 P13 P16	eq	The eq value with one of the filter operator parameters indicates that the filter should use the Equal To or Is In condition in the filter. A single value can be included in the Filter Value (P3, P6, P9, etc.) parameter by including just the filter value after the Filter Value tag. Multiple values may be used by using the n+values syntax described later.

TABLE 3-3. *Go URL Tags* (continued)

Tag	Values	Description
	neq	Using the neq value with one of the filter operator parameters indicates that the filter should use the Is Not Equal To or Not In condition in the filter. One or more values should be included in the filter value (P3, P6, P9, etc.) parameter.
	lt	Using the lt value with one of the filter operator parameters indicates that the filter should use the Is Less Than condition in the filter. A single value should be included in the filter value (P3, P6, P9, etc.) parameter.
	gt	Using the gt value with one of the filter operator parameters indicates that the filter should use the Is Greater Than condition in the filter. A single value should be included in the filter value (P3, P6, P9, etc.) parameter.
	ge	Using the ge value with one of the filter operator parameters indicates that the filter should use the Is Greater Than or Equal To condition in the filter. A single value should be included in the filter value (P3, P6, P9, etc.) parameter.
	le	Using the le value with one of the filter operator parameters indicates that the filter should use the Is Less Than or Equal To condition in the filter. A single value should be included in the filter value (P3, P6, P9, etc.) parameter.
	bwith	Using the bwith value with one of the filter operator parameters indicates that the filter should use the Begins With condition in the filter. A single value should be included in the filter value (P3, P6, P9, etc.) parameter.
	ewith	Using the ewith value with one of the filter operator parameters indicates that the filter should use the Ends With condition in the filter. A single value should be included in the filter value (P3, P6, P9, etc.) parameter.
	cany	Using the cany value with one of the filter operator parameters indicates that the filter should use the Contains Any condition in the filter. Multiple values should be included in the filter value (P3, P6, P9, etc.) parameter.

TABLE 3-3. *Go URL Tags* (continued)

Tag	Values	Description
	call	Using the call value with one of the filter operator parameters indicates that the filter should use the Contains All condition in the filter. Multiple values should be included in the filter value (P3, P6, P9, etc.) parameter.
	like	Using the like value with one of the filter operator parameters indicates that the filter should use the Is Like condition in the filter. The Is Like condition requires a value with a wildcard character, but the normal % character must be encoded as %25, for example.
	top	Using the top value with one of the filter operator parameters indicates that the filter should use the Is In Top condition in the filter. The filter value parameter should be a number.
	bottom	Using the bottom value with one of the filter operator parameters indicates that the filter should use the Is In Bottom condition in the filter. The filter value parameter should be a number.
	bet	Using the bet value with one of the filter operator parameters indicates that the filter should use the Is Between condition in the filter. The filter value parameter must contain two values (P3= 2+value1+value2).
	null	Using the null value with one of the filter operator parameters indicates that the filter should use the Is Null condition in the filter. The filter value parameter should be set to 0 or omitted.
	nnull	Using the nnull value with one of the filter operator parameters indicates that the filter should use the Is Not Null condition in the filter. The filter value parameter should be set to 0 or omitted.

TABLE 3-3.   *Go URL Tags* (continued)

Tag	Values	Description
P2 P5 P8 P11 P14 P17	Table.column	The Column parameter (P2, P5, P8, etc.) identifies the column in the report that you are filtering. This table.column reference must be the same as the column formula within the report that you have set with the Is Prompted filter. Special characters must be encoded using URL encoding. For instance, if applying a filter to the Number of Activities column, the analytic field reference of "Activity Metrics"."# of Activities" must be encoded and included in the URL as %22Activity+Metrics%22.%22%23+of+Activities%22, replacing " with %22, # with %23, and spaces with +.
P3 P6 P9 P12 P15 P18	filter value	The filter value parameter (P3, P6, P9, etc.) should contain the value or values being passed to the filter in the report using a syntax of n+value1+value2… where n is the number of values. If a single value is used, using 1+ before the value is optional. P3=2+100+500 is an example of the filter values for an Is Between filter with 100 as the first value and 500 as the second value. The values included in the URL can come from a few different places. They can be written directly into the URL as in the example, or they can be derived dynamically. A Web Link URL included on a record detail screen may include a value from a field on the current record in the URL. A report embedded inside of a narrative view in another report may include a value from the report by including a reference to the column in the filter value parameter. These methods are described later in this chapter.

TABLE 3-3. *Go URL Tags* (continued)

Not all links will require that you use the Go URL format. In some places, it is decidedly easier to create a link to a report. In the second half of this chapter, I describe the process for creating links to reports.

Linking Reports to Other Reports

One of the most common navigation requirements involving reports is to be able to navigate from one report to another, usually passing some filter values to the target report. Answers On Demand provides a navigate function that may be used to create this type of navigation. It is also possible to create links to other reports using a more manual process of building the Go URL within a column formula or narrative view in your report.

Navigate Function

The navigate functionality on report columns allows you to provide users with the ability to click on a value in order to run and possibly filter the current or another report. This is a highly flexible feature that allows you to create a series of reports that are all connected. You may also add multiple navigation targets to a single column. Many companies use this functionality to present data first at a high level and then navigate deeper and deeper into the data, moving from summary reports to detail reports.

Simple Navigation—No Filters

To establish a navigation path from one report to another, you will use the navigate interaction setting on the column and/or chart. To set up a navigate option on a report column, access the Column Properties window for the column on step 1 of the Build And View Analysis screen. On the Interaction tab, select the Navigate option in either of the Navigation Type fields. Upon selecting Navigate, the Add Navigation Target button appears beneath the field (Figure 3-3).

Click this button, and two new fields and two new buttons appear beneath the Add Navigation Target button (Figure 3-4). Click the Browse button to select a target report for the navigation. The selected report must be one that the user can normally access, given their visibility settings. The Caption field allows you to apply a custom caption to the navigation link. When you add more than one navigation target to a report, the user will see a pop-up menu when clicking the value in the report. The caption does not display if there is only one target. If you choose to leave the Caption field blank, the names of the target reports appear in the pop-up menu.

You are able to add navigation targets to both the column headings and column values. Navigation targets for the column headings and column

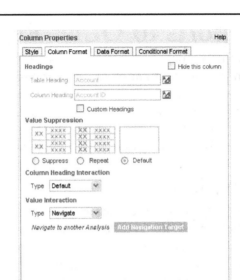

FIGURE 3-3. *Column Properties – Column Format with Add Navigation Target button*

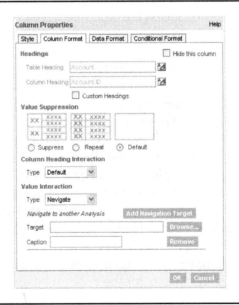

FIGURE 3-4. *Target navigation fields*

values do not need to be the same. The simple navigation I describe earlier runs another report, but does not necessarily pass any values from the linking report to the target report. The configuration of the navigate functionality is the same if you are passing filter values to the target report, but the target report must be expecting to receive a value. In order to use the navigate feature to run and filter another report, you must modify the target report to receive the clicked value that passes from the linking report.

Open the target report, which you will have created before setting up the navigate interaction. Add a filter to the column that contains the data you plan to pass from the linking report. Set the condition on the filter to Is Prompted. This filter setting will have no effect on your report unless a value is passed to it. You could place an Is Prompted filter on every column and that report would be unfiltered if a user runs it from the Reports tab. The same report, when the target of a column value navigate interaction, will filter to the records that equal the value clicked in the linking report.

The same target report with the same filter accessed through a navigate interaction on a column heading will run unfiltered. This means you can give your users the ability to filter the target report by clicking a value or simply run the target report unfiltered by clicking the linked column heading.

Use Navigate to Filter a Current Report

The target of your navigate interaction need not be another report. You can use the navigate interaction to filter the current report by placing the Is Prompted filter on the same column as you place a navigate interaction, targeting the very report you are adding the navigate interaction to. When a user runs the report from the Reports tab, the report is unfiltered because no value is passed to the filter. When the user then clicks one of the interactive values in the report, the same report runs again, only this time the clicked value passes to the column filter and the report shows only records with values that match the clicked value.

Navigating from Charts

You can also set up your charts with the navigate interaction. By clicking a value represented in the measure area of your chart, you may navigate to or navigate to and filter another report. To enable the navigate interaction on a chart, click the Additional Charting Options button on the Edit View Chart screen to open the Additional Charting Options window. On the Interaction tab of this window, click the Navigate option. The rest of the process is exactly like setting up navigation on a column. Click the Add Target Report button, and browse for and select a report for the Target field. Enter a caption in the Caption field if you want to display something other than the report name when more than one target report is defined.

Include a Report Hyperlink in a Formula

The purpose of a column formula in a report is to return a value from the CRM On Demand data. We often manipulate this value in some way or apply logic to display one value or another based on some sort of condition. Suppose you want to run a report filtered using a value that you have calculated in a report column formula. Using the navigate function does not really work out too well because the column formulas may not match exactly between the source and target reports. This is one reason we might want to construct the report hyperlink in a formula.

This method is not for the timid, mind you. You will need to create the hyperlink using a combination of HTML and report formula writing. Let us take an example where we want to link on the account name from our main report and filter the target report with that account name. This simple example is one that could be accomplished with the navigate function, but illustrates the process in as simple a fashion as possible.

In the main report, we replace the formula with the following string formula:

```
'<a href=/OnDemand/user/analytics/saw.dll?Go&Path=
%2fshared%2fCompany_ML1234-1BWB2_Shared_
Folder%2fActivityCount&Options=rfd&Action=Navigate&p0=1&p1=eq&p2=
Account.%22Account+Name%22&p3='||REPLACE(Account."Account Name",'
','+')||' target="_top">'||Account."Account Name"||'</a>'
```

This formula concatenates five strings to ultimately generate in each row the name of an account that is hyperlinked to an activity report filtered using the account name. The double pipe symbol included between each string is the concatenate function. The first string in this formula begins the hyperlink HTML, with the anchor tag and the portion of the Go URL up to the Filter Value parameter (P3=). This string is enclosed within single quotes, indicating that it is a text-literal value.

The next string provides the filter value. Because it is possible for this value to include spaces, the REPLACE function is used here to replace any spaces with a + character. Remember, the resulting URL can contain no spaces.

The third string continues the HTML anchor tag. Here we can include the optional target command to indicate in which window or frame the target of the hyperlink should be opened. We also include the > character to end the first portion of the anchor tag.

The fourth string in the formula is the formula that will return the account name. This could just as easily be a literal value, such as "Click Here," depending on your needs.

This portion of the formula indicates what should appear in the main report and has no effect on the hyperlink or filter.

Finally, the fifth string is the last bit of HTML to close the anchor tag. This must be inside of single quotes, as it is a literal-text value.

Of course, this is a simple example. You would not likely use this particular method if your navigation need is this simple. However, if you need to navigate from one report to another based on some sort of complex algorithm, this may be the only option you have. Suppose you want to link from one report to another based on the results of a case statement that assigns a value based on values from other columns. Such a link would require that the value included in the filter value parameter be dynamic based on the results of your case statement formula. Such a formula is shown here for your examination:

```
'<a href=/OnDemand/user/analytics/saw.dll?Go&Path=
%2fshared%2fCompany_ML1234-1BWB2_Shared_
Folder%2fActivityCount&Options=rfd&Action=Navigate&p0=1&p1=eq&p2=
Account.INDEXED_SHORTEXT_0&p3='||CASE WHEN Account.Industry IN
('Media & Entertainment', 'High Technology', 'Telecommunications')
THEN 'Technology' WHEN Account.Industry IN ('Manufacturing',
'Automotive') THEN 'Mechanical' ELSE 'Other' END||' target="_
top">'||View Activity by Industry Segment||'</a>'
```

The actual formula is only part of the solution with this type of navigation link. Because you are relying on some HTML code to generate the hyperlink in your report, you will need to format the column as HTML. Do this by clicking the Column Properties button on the column containing the link formula. On the Column Properties window, open the Data Format tab and select the Override Default Data Format check box. Change the Treat Text As value to HTML. Figure 3-5 shows the Data Format tab for the column set to HTML.

FIGURE 3-5. *Column Properties window – Data Format tab*

Include a Hyperlink in a Narrative View

You can also use HTML code inside of a narrative view in your report to add a hyperlink to another report. The narrative view is essentially an HTML frame inside of your report, so adding a hyperlink is a natural use of the narrative view. If we use the simple hyperlink example provided earlier and create the same link using the narrative view and the account name from the first column in our report, the link will appear as shown here in the narrative:

```
<a href=/OnDemand/user/analytics/saw.dll?Go&Path=
%2fshared%2fCompany_ML1234-1BWB2_Shared_
Folder%2fActivityCount&Options=rfd&Action=Navigate&p0=1&p1=eq&p2=
Account.%22Account+Name%22&p3=@2 target="_top">@1</a>
```

In this example, I have the account name in the first column of my report, and that value is referenced with @1 in the narrative view. Since the name of an account may include spaces, I have also included a column in my report that replaces the spaces in the account name with the + character.

I positioned this as my second column. This value is referenced with @2 in the narrative view. This second column is only necessary when the filter value contains spaces. The column may be hidden if you do not want it to appear in other views.

Linking Reports to Detail and Edit Screens

Another common navigation requirement is to move from a report to a record detail screen by clicking a record in a report. Answers On Demand provides an ActionLink functionality that can be used to navigate from a report to a record detail screen. The ActionLink works extremely well in the right situation, but has some distinct limitations. ActionLinks are only effective in the Table view and work for a handful of record types as described below. We can overcome these limitations by creating hyperlinks using a column formula. The URLs for the record detail screens are different from the Go URLs for reports. Next I describe both the ActionLink and the formula-based URLs that navigate your users from a report to a record detail screen.

ActionLinks

Using an ActionLink, users are able to navigate from a report to the detail record for a selected account, opportunity, contact, campaign, lead, service request, or user record. You configure columns with ActionLink functionality on step 1 of the Build And View Analysis screen. The first thing you will need to do in order to effectively enable an ActionLink is to insert the ID column for the object you are linking to. You will need to position this column to the immediate right of the column that will contain the link. Examine Figure 3-6. Notice that I have inserted the Account ID column to the immediate right of the Account Name column. I would most likely format the Account ID column as hidden in my report, but the ID column must be there in order to properly pass the ID to the URL that will take you to the detail screen for that record.

Next, you open the Column Properties window for the column containing the values you want to use as a link to the detail screen. On the Style tab, expand the Custom CSS Style Options (HTML Only) section to

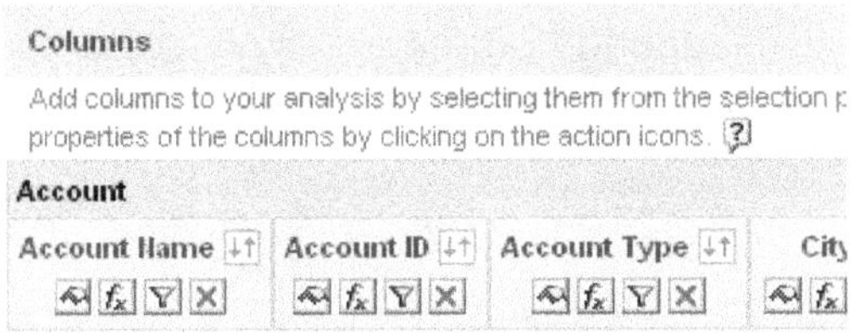

Columns

Add columns to your analysis by selecting them from the selection p
properties of the columns by clicking on the action icons. [?]

Account

Account Name ↓↑	Account ID ↓↑	Account Type ↓↑	City

FIGURE 3-6. *Account ID to right of Account Name column*

expose the Use Custom CSS Style and Use Custom CSS Class fields. Select
the Use Custom CSS Class check box and type **ActionLink** into the Use
Custom CSS Class field.

With the ActionLink CSS class on the column, the column values are
formatted as a link, and when a user clicks a value in the report, a URL is
dynamically generated using the text in that column and the ID column. On
the Data Format tab, you will change the format to Custom Text Format and
enter the ActionLink JavaScript code in the Custom Text Format field as
shown in Figure 3-7.

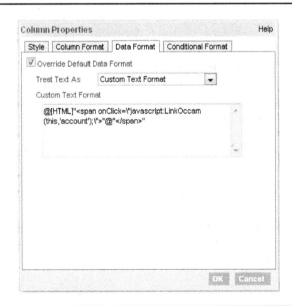

FIGURE 3-7. *Column Properties Window – Style Tab with ActionLink
Class*

The code for the ActionLink has a specific structure. Table 3-4 gives you the exact code that you should enter into the Custom Text Format field for each of the valid Action Class record types.

The resulting URL when a user clicks an action link has the following format:

```
/OnDemand/user/AccountDetail?OMTHD=AccountDetailNav&OMTGT=
AccountDetailForm&AccountDetailForm.Id=[ACCOUNT ID FROM NEXT
COLUMN]
```

The ActionLink functionality only works properly in the Table view and only for the primary record types listed earlier. If you want to create a navigation link from a report to one of the other record types, or if you need the link to work from within a pivot table, you will need to build the URL a little more manually.

Record Type	Custom Text Format JavaScript
Account	@[html]"<span onClick=\"javascript:LinkOccam (this,'account');\">"@"</span>"
Opportunity	@[html]"<span onClick=\"javascript:LinkOccam (this,'opportunity');\">"@"</span>"
Contact	@[html]"<span onClick=\"javascript:LinkOccam (this,'contact');\">"@"</span>"
Campaign	@[html]"<span onClick=\"javascript:LinkOccam (this,'campaign');\">"@"</span>"
Lead	@[html]"<span onClick=\"javascript:LinkOccam (this,'lead');\">"@"</span>"
Service Request	@[html]"<span onClick=\"javascript:LinkOccam (this,'service');\">"@"</span>"
User	@[html]"<span onClick=\"javascript:LinkOccam (this,'user');\">"@"</span>"

TABLE 3-4. *Action Link Text*

Custom Text Format Links

To create a link that works inside of a pivot table and links to objects that are not available with the ActionLink class like tasks and assets, you will need to build the URL using a custom text format.

As you would with an ActionLink, you need to add the ID column for the record type you are linking to. This time, the position does not matter, as we will be building the link on the ID column itself. Open the Column Properties window, and access the Data Format tab.

The text that you need to insert into the Custom Text Format field is largely the same as the URL that you see in the address bar of your browser when you access a detail screen in Oracle CRM On Demand. For example, a link to the Account Detail screen built on the Account ID column would be formatted as shown here and in Figure 3-8:

```
@[html]<a href="/OnDemand/user/AccountDetail?OMTGT=
AccountDetailForm&AccountDetailForm.Id="@ target="_blank">Account
Details</a>
```

FIGURE 3-8. *Column Properties – Data Format tab with account details link*

Table 3-5 describes the components of the Custom Text Format field necessary to build the URL for this type of link.

In Table 3-6 you see a sample custom text format for most of the record types available to you in Oracle CRM On Demand. The only portions of these codes that you can change without risk of rendering the link

Custom Text Segment	Description
@[html]	This indicates that the column text format is HTML
<a href="	This is the beginning of the HTML anchor tag.
/OnDemand/user/ AccountDetail?	Beginning of the URL. Notice that the http and secure server address portions of the URL are assumed and are not necessary for the link.
OMTGT=AccountDetailForm	The OMTGT tag identifies the target form of the URL.
&AccountDetailForm.Id="@	This portion of the code identifies the record ID. The @ character in this code instructs Oracle CRM On Demand to use the ID in the column of the clicked record. This is why we must use the object's ID column in the report for this link.
target="_blank">	The target tag can be one of four options. The value here indicates how you want the target form to open. target="_top" within a link tag causes the page to load in the entire current window. target="_parent" is similar to target="_top" but opens the page in the immediate parent of a frame. Within On Demand, parent and top are the same. target="_blank" causes the link to open in a new browser window, leaving the report still open behind it. target="_self" loads the page within the same frame as the link.
Account Details</a>	This final portion of the HTML hyperlink tag provides the display text for the link and closes the tag. If you place the @ character between the quotation marks, the hyperlink shows the contents of the report cell, which is the record ID.

TABLE 3-5.   *HTML Link Components*

Record Type	Custom Text Format Code
Account	@[html]<a href="/OnDemand/user/AccountDetail?OMTGT= AccountDetailForm&AccountDetailForm.Id="@ target="_ top">Account Details</a>
Opportunity	@[html]<a href="/OnDemand/user/OpportunityDetail?OMTGT= OpptyDetailForm&OpptyDetailForm.Id="@ target="_ top">Opportunity Details</a>
Contact	@[html]<a href="/OnDemand/user/ContactDetail?OMTGT= ContactDetailForm &ContactDetailForm.Id="@ target="_ top">Contact Details</a>
Campaign	@[html]<a href="/OnDemand/user/CampaignDetail?OMTGT= CampaignDetailForm&CampaignDetailForm.Id="@ target="_ top">Campaign Details</a>
Lead	@[html]<a href="/OnDemand/user/LeadsDetailPage?OMTGT= LeadDetailForm &LeadDetailForm.Id="@ target="_top">Lead Details</a>
Service Request	@[html]<a href="/OnDemand/user/ServiceRequestDetail?OMTGT= ServiceRequestDetailForm&ServiceRequestDetailForm.Id="@ target="_top">SR Details</a>
User	@[html]<a href="/OnDemand/user/AppDrillDwnUserDetail?OMTGT= UserDetailForm&UserDetailForm.Id="@ target="_top">User Details</a>
Task	@[html]<a href="/OnDemand/user/TaskDetail?OMTGT= TaskDetailForm&TaskDetailForm.Id="@ target="_top">Task Details</a>
Appointment	@[html]<a href="/OnDemand/user/ApptDetail?&OMTGT= ApptDetailForm&ApptDetailForm.Id="@ target="_ parent">Appointment Details</a>
Asset	@[html]<a href="/OnDemand/user/AssetDetail?OMTGT= AssetDetailForm&AssetDetailForm.Id="@ target="_top">Asset Details</a>
Product	@[html]<a href="/OnDemand/user/ProductDetail?OMTGT= ProductDetailForm&ProductDetailForm.Id="@ target="_ top">Product Details</a>

TABLE 3-6. *Custom Format Text for Detail Form Links*

Record Type	Custom Text Format Code
Custom Object 1	@[html]<a href="/OnDemand/user/CustomObj1Detail?OMTGT= CustObj1DetailForm&CustObj1DetailForm.Id="@ target="_ top">Details</a>
Custom Object 2	@[html]<a href="/OnDemand/user/CustomObj2Detail?OMTGT= CustObj2DetailForm&CustObj2DetailForm.Id="@ target="_ top">Details</a>
Custom Object 3	@[html]<a href="/OnDemand/user/CustomObj3Detail?OMTGT= CustObj3DetailForm&CustObj3DetailForm.Id="@ target="_ top">Details</a>
Custom Object 4	@[html]<a href="/OnDemand/user/CustomObject4.Detail?OMTGT= CustomObject4.Detail&CustomObject4.Detail.Id="@ target="_ top">Details</a>
Custom Object 5	@[html]<a href="/OnDemand/user/CustomObject5.Detail?OMTGT= CustomObject5.Detail&CustomObject5.Detail.Id="@ target="_ top">Details</a>
Custom Object 6	@[html]<a href="/OnDemand/user/CustomObject6.Detail?OMTGT= CustomObject6.Detail&CustomObject6.Detail.Id="@ target="_ top">Details</a>
Custom Object 7	@[html]<a href="/OnDemand/user/CustomObject7.Detail?OMTGT= CustomObject7.Detail&CustomObject7.Detail.Id="@ target="_ top">Details</a>
Custom Object 8	@[html]<a href="/OnDemand/user/CustomObject8.Detail?OMTGT= CustomObject8.Detail&CustomObject8.Detail.Id="@ target="_ top">Details</a>
Custom Object 9	@[html]<a href="/OnDemand/user/CustomObject9.Detail?OMTGT= CustomObject9.Detail&CustomObject9.Detail.Id="@ target="_ top">Details</a>
Custom Object 10	@[html]<a href="/OnDemand/user/CustomObject10.Detail?OMTGT= CustomObject10.Detail&CustomObject10.Detail.Id="@ target="_ top">Details</a>

TABLE 3-6.   *Custom Format Text for Detail Form Links* (continued)

Record Type	Custom Text Format Code
Custom Object 11	@[html]<a href="/OnDemand/user/CustomObject11.Detail?OMTGT= CustomObject11.Detail&CustomObject11.Detail.Id="@ target="_ top">Details</a>
Custom Object 12	@[html]<a href="/OnDemand/user/CustomObject12.Detail?OMTGT= CustomObject12.Detail&CustomObject12.Detail.Id="@ target="_ top">Details</a>
Custom Object 13	@[html]<a href="/OnDemand/user/CustomObject13.Detail?OMTGT= CustomObject13.Detail&CustomObject13.Detail.Id="@ target="_ top">Details</a>
Custom Object 14	@[html]<a href="/OnDemand/user/CustomObject14.Detail?OMTGT= CustomObject14.Detail&CustomObject14.Detail.Id="@ target="_ top">Details</a>
Custom Object 15	@[html]<a href="/OnDemand/user/CustomObject15.Detail?OMTGT= CustomObject15.Detail&CustomObject15.Detail.Id="@ target="_ top">Details</a>

TABLE 3-6. *Custom Format Text for Detail Form Links* (continued)

nonfunctional are the last two components. You may adjust the target and the display text as described earlier.

You will notice from the link structures in Table 3-3 that these URLs are a simplified version of the URLs you normally encounter in Oracle CRM On Demand. If you examine the URL from the Address field in your browser while accessing a record detail screen, you will see quite a few more tags that are technically necessary to navigate to the screen. Some of these tags contain information about where the user came from and, if you are using dynamic layouts, the name of the record type that drives the layout.

The OCTYPE tag identifies the value from the picklist field that drives the dynamic layout for the record. If you are navigating to a detail screen with a dynamic layout, you will need to pass the record ID value and the record type value in the URL. Given this situation, you will not be able to use the Custom Text Format method. If you need to include multiple values in the URL, you will need to construct the hyperlink using a custom string formula.

Formula Links

Links to Oracle CRM On Demand detail screens may be built using a string formula in a similar manner as described earlier in this chapter for links to reports. The need to pass multiple values for dynamic layouts is generally the reason for wanting to use a formula to build a link to a detail screen.

You will build your hyperlink using a combination of HTML and report formula writing. A link to an opportunity detail record that is a new business opportunity type, for instance, would need to include the opportunity ID and the opportunity type in order to navigate to the correct record and call the correct screen layout.

In the report, you would include the following formula:

```
'<a href=/OnDemand/user/OpportunityDetail?OMTGT=
OpptyDetailForm&OpptyDetailForm.Id='||Opportunity."Opportunity ID"||
'&OCTYPE='||REPLACE(Opportunity."Sales Type", ' ', '+')||' target=
"top">'||Opportunity.Name||'</a>'
```

This formula concatenates seven strings to ultimately generate in each row the name of an opportunity that is hyperlinked to the detail screen for that record. The double pipe symbol included between each string is the concatenate function. The first string in this formula begins the hyperlink HTML with the anchor tag and the portion of the detail screen URL up to the record ID field. This string is enclosed within single quotes, indicating that it is a text-literal value.

The next string provides the value from the Opportunity ID field. The REPLACE function is not needed here because the record ID values in Oracle CRM On Demand do not include spaces.

The third string adds the OCTYPE tag to the URL. This tag contains is used to identify the record type, in this case, opportunity type. This is necessary when navigating to a detail screen that is relying on the Type column to determine the correct layout. If you are not using a dynamic layout for the record type you are linking to, this tag is not needed.

The fourth string in the formula calls the value from the Opportunity Type column. The REPLACE function is needed here to ensure spaces are encoded properly.

The fifth string finishes off the first half of the anchor HTML tag, including the optional target, specifying that the screen should open in the same window as the report.

The sixth string calls the opportunity name. This is what will actually display in the report as the hyperlinked text. This could just as easily be a literal value, such as "Opportunity Details," if you prefer.

Finally, the seventh string is the last bit of HTML to close the anchor tag. This must be inside single quotes, as it is a literal-text value.

Because you are relying on some HTML code to generate the hyperlink in your report, you will need to format the column as HTML, previously illustrated in Figure 3-5.

Hyperlink in a Narrative

You can also use HTML code inside of a narrative view in your report to add a hyperlink to a detail screen. Using the Opportunity Detail hyperlink example shown earlier, the same link using the narrative view is shown here. This is assuming that we have included the opportunity ID in the first column, the opportunity type (with spaces replaced with +) in the second column, and the opportunity name in the third.

```
<a href=/OnDemand/user/OpportunityDetail?OMTGT=
OpptyDetailForm&OpptyDetailForm.Id=@1&OCTYPE=@2 target="top">@3</a>
```

Links to Edit Screens

Open any record homepage in Oracle CRM On Demand and click the New button to create a new record. In the Address field of your browser you will find the URL for the Record Edit screen. The basic Edit screen URL is quite simple and can be included in your reports using a narrative view or formula just like the detail screen URLs, except you do not need to worry about passing record values to the URL.

A typical HTML hyperlink to the Account Edit screen URL for a new account is shown here:

```
<a href=/OnDemand/user/DefAccountInsert?OMTGT=
AccountEditForm&OMTHD=AccountNewNav>New Account</a>
```

New records are quite simple since there are no record values that need to be included in the URL. A link to the Edit screen for an existing record, on the other hand, is quite a bit more complex. The formula for generating an Edit hyperlink for an opportunity record is shown here. Notice that this formula, while similar in structure to the detail screen URLs, requires that the record ID be included in the URL a couple of times, and in the case of dynamic layouts, the record type should also be included.

```
'<a href=/OnDemand/user/
OpptyCreateEditPage?OMTGT%3dOpptyDetailForm%26OMTHD%3dOpportunity
DetailNav%26OpptyDetailForm.Id%3d'||Opportunity."Opportunity ID"||
'%26ocEdit%3dY&OpptyCreateEditForm.Id='||Opportunity."Opportunity
ID"||'&OMTGT=OpptyCreateEditForm&OMTHD=OpportunityEditNav&OCTYPE='||
REPLACE(Opportunity."Sales Type", ' ', '+')||'>Edit</a>'
```

So, it is hopefully becoming clear to you that it is possible to build hyperlinks from your reports to nearly any screen in Oracle CRM On Demand, although it may take some trial and error to get the exact URL worked out. Each URL is unique, and there are certainly too many to include examples of each in this book, but with a little practice and these examples, you should be able to work out the format for any link you need.

Web Link Fields

A user with administrative access in Oracle CRM On Demand is able to create custom fields on the different objects. One of the field types available is the Web Link field. A Web Link field on a page layout provides a hyperlink that can link to another webpage, either another Oracle On Demand screen or an external site. The special thing about the Web Link field is that you are able to insert record values inside of the target URL identified in the Web Link. This feature is often used to provide a link on a detail screen to access a report that is filtered using the current record.

The basic steps for creating a Web Link field are listed here. Not all options are explained here, as they are generally not needed for report links, but it is possible to apply some logic around how the links are displayed using expressions. That functionality is beyond the scope of this book, but I encourage you to explore the possibilities.

If you have trouble with this process or do not have the necessary access to create new fields and layouts, consult with your Oracle CRM On Demand administrator for assistance.

1. Click the Admin Global link.

2. Click the Application Customization link.

3. Click a Record Type link in the Record Type Setup section.

4. Click a Field Setup link for the selected record type.

5. Click New Field button.

6. Complete the Display Name field, select Web Link in the Field Type field, and click Save.

7. Click the Edit Web Link link next to the new field in the list to access the Edit Web Link window (Figure 3-9).

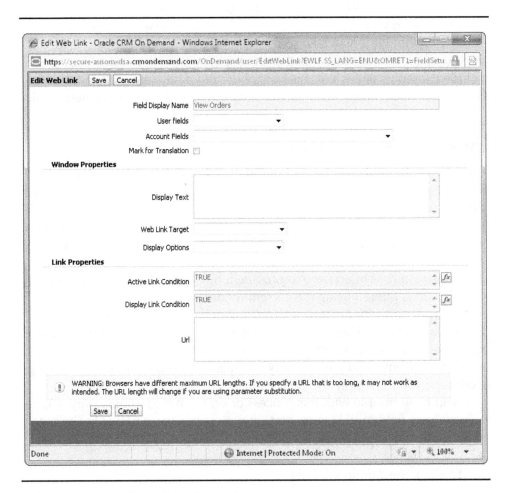

FIGURE 3-9. *Edit Web Link window*

8. In the Window Properties section, enter the text you want to appear on the screen layout in the Display Text field.

9. Select the way your target page should open in the Web Link Target field.

10. In the Display Options field, indicate whether the link should appear on the Detail page, Edit page, or both.

11. Enter the Go URL for the report into the URL field. The user fields and record type fields drop-down lists insert field references in the URL field for passing values to the URL for the filter value parameters if filtering the target report.

12. After completing the screen, click the Save button.

13. Click the Back To Application Customization link.

14. Click the Page Layout link.

15. Click the Edit link next to the layout onto which you want to add your Web Link.

16. Access step 3 of the wizard, and locate your Web Link field in the list on the left side of the screen. Use the arrow buttons to position your field on the layout.

17. Click Finish.

Your completed Web Link URL will appear something like the URL shown here. This particular URL is passing two values to a report with different conditions. One requirement here is that you must include the generic host of https://secure.crmondemand.com in the URL.

```
https://secure.crmondemand.com/OnDemand/user/analytics/
saw.dll?Go&Path=%2fshared%2fCompany_ML1234-1BWB2_Shared_
Folder%2fAccountInformation&Options=rfd&Action=Navigate&P0=2&P1=
eq&P2=Account."Account Region"&P3=%%%Region%%%&P4=gt&P5=
Account."Number of Employees"&P6=500
```

The Account Region value in this URL is inserted by selecting the field from the Account Fields drop-down list in the Edit Web Link window. Values inserted into the Web Link from the record are prefixed and suffixed with three percent characters. Account region is, in this case, %%%Region%%%.

Dashboard Links

A dashboard is a webpage that may contain many different elements. Most people think about dashboards containing embedded reports, and that is certainly the most common use of a dashboard. I briefly discuss embedded reports in a dashboard in the next chapter. Reports are not the only elements that you can include in your dashboards, however. One of the objects that you can include in your dashboard is the Link or Image object. With this element on your dashboard, you can create links to other webpages and reports. You can also embed a report as a link rather than displaying the report.

In addition to linking from a dashboard, you may want to include a link from another location in Oracle CRM On Demand into a dashboard. I describe this link in this section as well. If you find yourself working with dashboards extensively, you may want to pick up a copy of *Oracle CRM On Demand Dashboards* (McGraw-Hill/Professional, 2010) in which I describe dashboards in Oracle CRM On Demand in greater detail. The explanations here assume you are already familiar with basic dashboard development.

Linking from a Dashboard

The Link or Image Object provides the capability to display a hyperlink to another website URL or a specific report in the report library. This object also allows you to display an image on your dashboard. The image can also be made clickable to navigate to the specified URL or report. To add a Link or Image Object to your dashboard, drag the desired link or image from the list of dashboard objects to a section on your dashboard layout in the Dashboard Editor screen. Dropping a link or image object onto your dashboard generates no results until you have modified the properties of the object.

Properties

Click the Properties button on the link or image object to open the Link Or Image Properties window shown in Figure 3-10. By completing some or all of these fields, you can create a number of different elements on your dashboard. You can create a text link, image link, or both that, when clicked, can open a webpage or report from the Oracle CRM On Demand report library. You can also include just text or just an image without the link to another page or report. You can create a link, add a text caption, and add an image (these last two are optional).

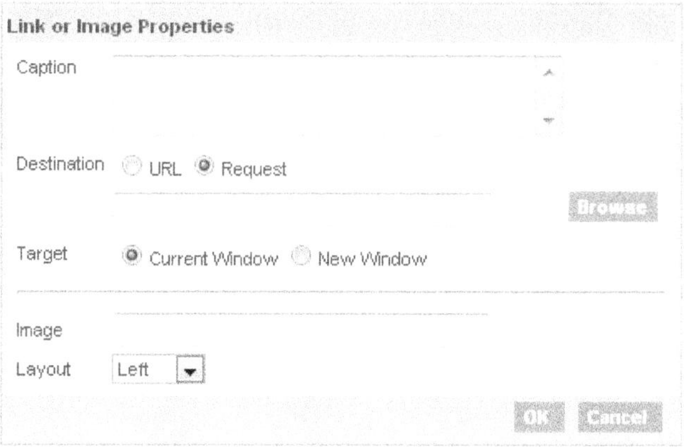

FIGURE 3-10.   *Link or Image Properties window*

To create a text link, you will want to enter some text into the Caption field. The text you enter here will be the text that appears on the dashboard as a hyperlink. Below the Caption field, you find two options. These are used to identify the type of destination that your link is going to take dashboard users to when they click it. The first option is URL. This option allows you to access any webpage as long as you know the URL for it. For instance, if you want to provide a link to your company homepage from the dashboard, you would select the URL Destination option and enter the full URL in the Destination field. The http:// portion of the URL is required.

You can also use a mailto URL here to create a link that initiates a new e-mail message. Enter a URL like mailto:mike@email.net?subject= Dashboard, and the resulting hyperlink in the dashboard, when clicked, will open the user's default e-mail application and create a new message addressed to mike@email.net with a subject of Dashboard.

Your other Destination option on the Link Or Image Properties window is Request. This is referring to a report request in Oracle CRM On Demand. Select the Request option, and rather than enter a URL in the Destination field, you will browse for the desired report. Click the Browse button, and the Choose Request window opens with the Company Wide Shared Folder and Pre-built Analysis folders listed. Drill down into the folders and select a report. Notice that your personal report folder is not an available option. When you click OK, the URL for the selected report appears in the Destination field.

Next up is the target selection. The results of your link can be opened in either the current window, replacing the dashboard, or in a new browser window. To open a report or URL in the same window as the dashboard, select the Current Window option. The target page of the hyperlink opens within the dashboard window below the Select Dashboard field. If your destination is a report request, a hyperlink is positioned at the bottom of the resulting window that returns you to the dashboard. Click the Return link, and you are taken right back to the dashboard window from whence you came. A Return link is not provided for the results of links from the dashboard to a URL.

Select the New Window option, and your hyperlinked report or URL will open in a new browser window. The dashboard remains open in your browser.

If you want to include an image on your dashboard, you enter the URL for it in the Image field on the Link Or Image Properties window. This URL needs to be the full URL with the http:// or https:// prefix and filename for the image. If a partial URL is entered here, it is appended to /OnDemandContent/user/analytics. The image must be located on a web server that the dashboard user has access to. An image located behind a firewall, for instance, would be unavailable to a user working from outside the network. The image also needs to be in a format that is displayable within a web browser.

The Layout field allows you to position the caption relative to the image. This is a bit counterintuitive since the Layout field is located with the Image field rather than the Caption field, but the Layout option actually describes the location of the caption as it relates to the image. Your options are Above, Below, Left, and Right. Selecting Above positions the caption above the image.

Breakout Link

Often, the available real estate on the dashboard screen is just not enough to do what you want to do. One potential solution is to add a link to the dashboard that opens the same dashboard in a new window, without the CRM On Demand user interface objects like the page tabs and Action bar. The most difficult part of creating this link on your dashboard is discovering the correct URL for the dashboard.

Begin by saving your dashboard and accessing the Dashboard tab. It is important that you open the dashboard on the Dashboard tab and not the preview window that appears when you save the dashboard. Once the dashboard is loaded on the Dashboard tab, and before you click anything else, right-click the blue bar below the Select Dashboard field. Note the location of the cursor in Figure 3-11. If your dashboard contains multiple pages, right-click the blue bar to the right of the tabs. Do not navigate to any of the other pages in the dashboard before right-clicking the blue bar on the dashboard page.

When you right-click the dashboard, the right-click menu appears. Select Properties if you are using Internet Explorer; select This Frame and then View Frame Info if you are using Firefox. On the resulting window, highlight and copy the contents of the Address field to your Clipboard.

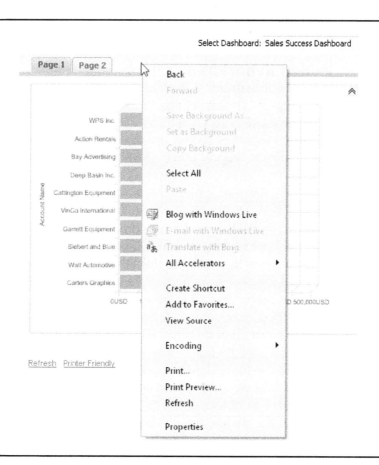

FIGURE 3-11. *Locating the dashboard frame URL*

This is the address for the dashboard content inside the dashboard frame, and is the link you will add to your dashboard to break the dashboard out of the frame and open it into a new browser window.

The address URL will look something like the following example. Note that some characters may be URL-encoded, so a / may be represented as %2f.

```
https://secure-ausomxdsa.crmondemand.com/OnDemand/user/analytics/
saw.dll?Dashboard&PortalPath=/shared/Company_123456-1ABC2_Shared_
Folder/_portal/Marketing+Quarterly+Initiatives.
```

Once you have located the correct URL and have copied it to your Clipboard, you can go back to your Dashboard Editor screen and add the link or image object to your layout and paste in the URL. Be sure to provide a caption in the Caption field and select the New Window target.

Add an Embedded Report as a Link

Add a report to your dashboard by locating and dragging the report to your dashboard from the Shared Content section to the dashboard layout. On the report object within the dashboard layout you will find three buttons in the upper-right corner. The Properties button opens the Properties menu with four options: Display Results, Report Links, Show View, and Modify Request.

The first option in the Properties menu on the Report object is actually a submenu with three options. There are three different ways to display a report in a dashboard. The default, and most common, method is to embed the report in the section so that the report displays as part of the dashboard. You can also set your reports to display as links that, when clicked, open the report in the dashboard window or in a separate window. The two link options are the ones we are interested in here.

The Link – Within The Dashboard option is really very much the same as adding a link or image object that directs the user to a report in Oracle CRM On Demand. Adding a report to your dashboard and setting the Display Results property to Link – Within The Dashboard displays a link to the report, just like the link you would get from adding the link or image object or the guided navigation link object. Clicking the link in the dashboard replaces the contents of the dashboard window with the report results. Adding a report to your dashboard and displaying the dashboard as a link still counts as a report and, therefore, uses one of the six available spots for reports on the dashboard page. If you are pushing up against the six-report limit on your dashboard page, you might consider using one of the other link objects rather than a report.

The Link – In A Separate Window option is also similar to adding a link or image object that directs the user to a report in Oracle CRM On Demand, and is set to open in a new window. Adding a report to your dashboard and setting the Display Results property to Link – In A Separate Window displays a link to the report that looks exactly like the link you would get when adding the link or image object. Clicking the link in the dashboard opens a new window populated with the report results.

Linking to a Dashboard

The breakout link described earlier technically applies a link to a dashboard as well as a link from a dashboard, and as such, the method described earlier for locating the dashboard URL applies here. The URL for the dashboard can be included in Web Link fields and reports, just as you would when linking to a report.

The dashboard URL also accepts a couple of optional tags, as described in Table 3-7.

URL Tag	Description and Example
&Page=	Append the name of a specific dashboard page to navigate directly to that page of the dashboard. /OnDemand/user/analytics/ saw.dll?Dashboard&PortalPath= %2fshared%2fCompany_AA1234-1JAZ2_Shared_ Folder%2f_portal%2fSales&Page=Contacts
&Action=Print	Include the Action=Print tag at the end of the URL to open the dashboard directly in a printer-friendly window. This may be combined with the Page tag to open a specific dashboard page in a printer-friendly window. /OnDemand/user/analytics/ saw.dll?Dashboard&PortalPath= %2fshared%2fCompany_AA1234-1JAZ2_Shared_ Folder%2f_portal%2fSales&Action=Print

TABLE 3-7.   *Dashboard URL Tags*

Linking to a Filtered Dashboard

If your dashboard contains a dashboard filter prompt and you want to pass a value to your dashboard filter prompt as you navigate to the dashboard, you are able to use the same Action=Navigate tag followed by the filter parameters. The example here is a URL you might include in a Web Link field on an account detail screen that navigates to the Sales Dashboard, filtering the dashboard with the name of the current account record. If adding to a Web Link, be sure to include the generic host (https://secure .crmondemand.com) in the URL.

```
/OnDemand/user/analytics/saw.dll?Dashboard&PortalPath=
%2fshared%2fCompany_AA1234-1JAZ2_Shared_Folder%2f_
portal%2fSales&Action=Navigate&P0=1&P1=eq&P2=
Account.%22Account+Name%22&P3=%%%Name%%%
```

Special Links

I want to finish up this chapter on report navigation links with a few special link types that you might include in your reports or other places in Oracle CRM On Demand. E-mail links and external links can be included in your reports using the same methods as mentioned previously in this chapter, but there is also a data format setting that can make including these links much easier. Finally, links to web tabs are also quite similar, but require the full URL, including the host server.

E-mail Links

E-mail links that open the user's default e-mail application with a specified e-mail address can be included in a report using the standard mailto link format as shown here. This can be included using a string formula in a report formatted as HTML or as part of your HTML code in a narrative view.

```
<a href=mailto:mike@email.net?subject=Opportunity></a>
```

If the e-mail address you want to include in your mailto link is an actual value in a column within Oracle CRM On Demand, formatting the e-mail address as a link is quite easy. Add the e-mail address column to your report, and select the Mail-To Address value in the Treat Text As field. This changes the Custom Text Format field to @[html]"<a href="mailto:"@H"">"@"</a>", which adds the HTML anchor tag code around the e-mail address value from the column and displays the e-mail address as a hyperlink. The Subject tag is not included.

If you want to include a predetermined subject in your e-mail when using an e-mail address column in your report, you can do so by selecting the Custom Text Format value in the Treat Text As field and changing the Custom Text Format code to include the subject tag. I used an underscore character in my subject of Customer_Inquiry rather than a space because the space breaks the link.

```
@[html]"<a href="mailto:@?subject=Customer_Inquiry">"@"</a>"
```

Alternatively, if you want to display something other than the e-mail address as the hyperlink text, you can change the third @ in the Custom Text Format code to the text of your choosing. The following code results in an e-mail link that appears as "E-mail Customer" on the report. The space is acceptable in the hyperlink text here because it is not part of the actual hyperlink.

```
@[html]"<a href="mailto:@?subject=Customer_Inquiry">"E-mail
Customer"</a>"
```

External Links

You also have a custom text format for hyperlink text at your disposal for those website columns in your reports. Suppose you want to make a customer's website available to your report users with a hyperlink in the report. Add the website column to the report and change the data format of the column. This time, you want to select either HyperText Link or HyperText Link (Prepend http://) in the Treat Text As field. If your website column already includes the http:// prefix, you would select HyperText Link.

The HyperText Link (Prepend http://) option changes the Custom Text Format code as follows:

```
"http://"@[html]"<a href="http://"@H"">"@"</a>"
```

This changes the format of the text to HTML and adds the anchor tag code around the website address value in the report column. The value is included as the hyperlink text. Alternatively, if you want to display something other than the website address as the hyperlink text, you can change the third @ in the Custom Text Format code to the text of your choosing. The following code results in a hyperlink that appears as on the report as "Visit Website":

```
"http://"@[html]"<a href="http://"@H"">"Visit Website"</a>"
```

Of course, you can also use the techniques described earlier in this chapter to build hyperlinks to external sites. For example, if you wanted to include a link in your report that takes the user to an Internet search page and automatically executes a search on the company name of the record, you can write a column formula like the one here. Change the column data format to HTML, and you have a clickable search link in your report that searches on the account name.

```
'<a href=http://www.google.com/#hl=en&q='||REPLACE(Account."Account
Name", ' ', '+')||'>Search</a>'
```

Web Tab Links

Finally, we come to links to custom web tabs. Creating links to web tabs in Oracle CRM On Demand is almost exactly the same as linking to any other screen within the application. The primary difference here is that the URL must contain the specific host. This is different from the generic host you must include in other Web Link URLs. The URL for a custom web tab will be visible in your browser's Address field. The entire URL must be used to link to the web tab. Linking to a custom web tab is actually a rather common request, especially when that custom web tab has a report or dashboard embedded within it. Explore embedding reports more in the next chapter.

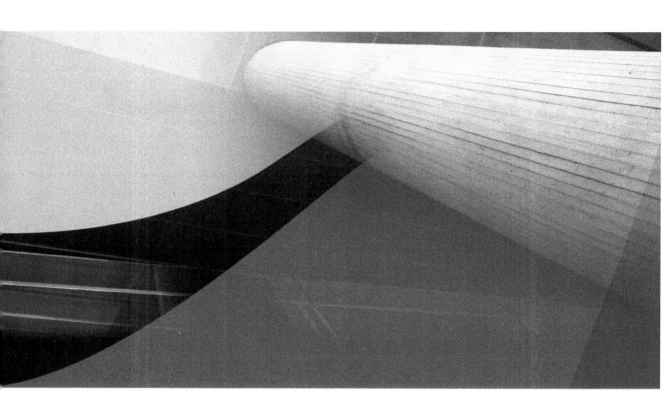

CHAPTER

4

Embedding Reports

here are several options for embedding reports in Oracle CRM On Demand. By embedded reports, I am referring to the practice of displaying the report, rather than a link, in places other than the Reports tab in Oracle CRM On Demand. Like the Column Interaction Navigate function described in the previous chapter, there are some methods for embedding reports that are provided in Oracle CRM On Demand as standard functionality. These are quite simple, and do not require a detailed knowledge of report URLs. Other methods are more manually configured and will require use of HTML and URL encoding.

In this chapter, I describe each of the different methods for embedding a report in Oracle CRM On Demand. I will begin with these basic methods for embedding reports, which include displaying reports inside of a dashboard and adding reports to your homepage screens.

In the last chapter I spent a lot of time describing the unique URLs that reference reports and screens in Oracle CRM On Demand. You will use many of those same URLs when embedding reports. Since we examined the URL structures in the last chapter, there is no need to repeat that information, but if you skipped that part of the book, please take the time to read through the information on report URLs before continuing.

The possibilities of how embedded reports can benefit your company and users are plentiful. The common enhancement to your business processes that embedded reports offer is a reduction in the amount of effort it takes to access information. The objective is for that information to be necessary and useful in that moment that the user sees the report presented on the screen.

The purpose behind reports is usually the dissemination of information, but people are, by nature, a bit lazy when it comes to retrieving the information. So often I see user adoption issues, where a library of fantastic reports has been developed but the users working with the application carry on with their normal routine and either forget to or just don't care to go to the Reports tab and locate a report that is designed to help them perform their tasks.

Embedding reports is an effective weapon against this type of apathy. The remainder of this chapter describes a number of techniques that you can use to put reports and analytics in front of your users without requiring them to remember or want to dig up the report on their own.

Reports on the Home Tab

You have likely noticed that all of the record-specific homepage tabs, as well as the Home tab in Oracle CRM On Demand, include a chart or some sort of report. Unless you or another administrator removed them, the default homepage layouts all have embedded within them a small report from the collection of pre-built reports. Reports you embed on homepages and elsewhere throughout the application are generally simple reports that contain a single view. This is because it is usually desirable when designing a report for a homepage, or for a web applet, to deliver a single meaningful view of data that summarizes a key indicator for a particular type of record.

When you design a report that you intend to embed on a homepage, there are a few considerations that you should account for in your design. First, consider the data for a homepage report. A report on a homepage should be general enough to apply to a set of records rather than a specific record. In other words, it does not make sense to filter a homepage report down to a specific record since you intend to display the report on a screen that is not specific to a single record. You may, however, want to filter the report to only include the current year, or current quarter, or some other restricted timeframe. You might also consider limiting the report data to the records that are owned by the current user or current manager. Making the report specific to a particular owner or particular timeframe can make the report more meaningful and useful while still providing a high-level summary appropriate for a homepage.

You should also consider the layout of the report. Every report contains a Title view and a Table view by default. Your reports are not required to display either of these views. For a report that you plan to deliver on a homepage, you may want to remove these two views and include only a chart or a pivot table. Generally, the simplest message is the best for a homepage report. Save the detailed analyses for your drill-down reports, and provide just a snapshot of data in a well-designed view on your homepages.

Another consideration is access to the report and the data therein. Be sure your users have the necessary access to the report and that the report displays the appropriate data based on visibility settings. It is possible to assign a different homepage layout to every role in Oracle CRM On Demand. Each layout can have different reports embedded, giving you another layer of flexibility in what data is presented to whom on the homepages.

Embedding reports onto your homepage screens does require administrative access in Oracle CRM On Demand. To embed a report on a homepage, click the Admin link to access the Admin homepage. Click Application Customization to access the Application Customization screen. From here you may select the My Custom Homepage Report link to make a report available on the main Homepage screen, or drill into a record type and select the Homepage Custom Report link to add a report to that particular record type homepage. Either path will take you to a list screen, where you can see a listing of any existing homepage reports. On this screen, click the New Homepage Report button to access the Homepage Custom Report Detail screen (Figure 4-1).

On this screen, you will begin by naming the homepage report. Of course, your report already has a name, and what you enter on this screen does not change that. The name you enter here on the Homepage Custom Report Detail screen is the name that will appear in the section heading on the homepage above your report.

The next two fields on this screen allow you to select the amount of screen real estate that your report will occupy on the homepage. You have the option of Single or Double in both the Height and Width fields. A report

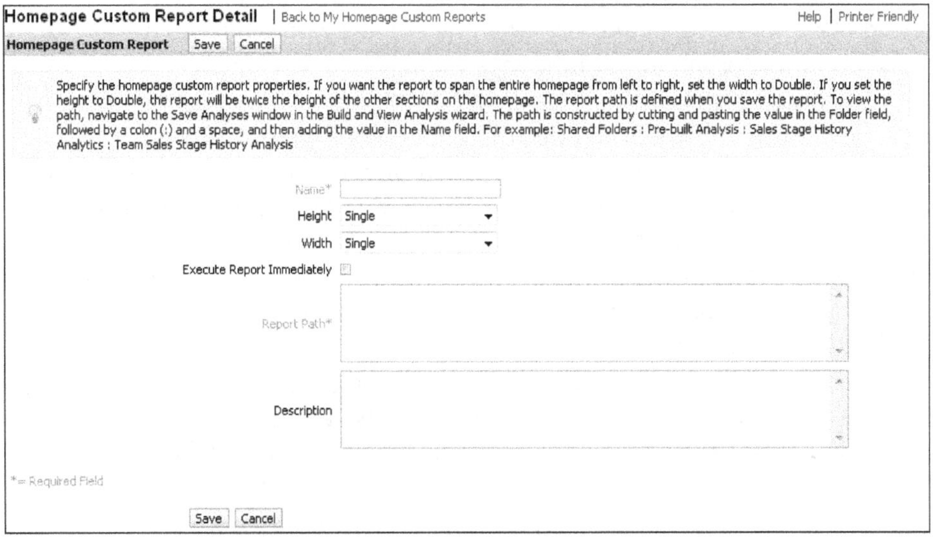

Homepage Custom Report Detail | Back to My Homepage Custom Reports   Help | Printer Friendly

Homepage Custom Report   Save   Cancel

Specify the homepage custom report properties. If you want the report to span the entire homepage from left to right, set the width to Double. If you set the height to Double, the report will be twice the height of the other sections on the homepage. The report path is defined when you save the report. To view the path, navigate to the Save Analyses window in the Build and View Analysis wizard. The path is constructed by cutting and pasting the value in the Folder field, followed by a colon (:) and a space, and then adding the value in the Name field. For example: Shared Folders : Pre-built Analysis : Sales Stage History Analytics : Team Sales Stage History Analysis

Name*

Height   Single

Width   Single

Execute Report Immediately

Report Path*

Description

* = Required Field

Save   Cancel

FIGURE 4-1. *Homepage Custom Report Detail screen*

set to double width will span the entire homepage from left to right. A report set to single width will only span one column of the homepage. A report set to double height will be twice the height of the other sections on the homepage screen, while a single-height report will be the same height as other sections.

The Execute Report Immediately check box controls how the report loads when the homepage is accessed. When this check box is selected, your homepage report will load immediately upon accessing the homepage screen. This is usually the most favorable option for user acceptance, but may cause the screen to load a bit slower than normal, depending on the complexity of the report. When this check box is left unselected, Oracle CRM On Demand does not attempt to load the report when the hosting homepage is accessed, but rather displays a link that allows the user to generate the report by clicking the "Generating Analysis.... Click here to view the results" hyperlink.

The path of the report is based on where you save the report. You will enter the path to the report using the following syntax:

```
Company Wide Shared Folder : <folder name> : <report name>
```

You can include multiple folders as needed to identify the location of the report. For example, a report named Quarterly Sales located in the Company Wide Shared Folder/Management Reports/Sales Reports folder has a path as follows:

```
Company Wide Shared Folder : Management Reports : Sales Reports :
Quarterly Sales
```

One way to determine the exact path to your report is to look in the Folder field when you are saving the report. You can copy and paste the value in the Folder field, followed by a colon and a space, and then type the name of the report shown in the Name field.

The Description field on the Homepage Custom Report Detail screen allows you to enter a description for the homepage report. The description is not displayed anywhere other than the list of homepage reports.

Once saved, the homepage report is available to be added to the homepage layout. To add a report to a homepage layout, return to the Application Customization screen. Click the My Homepage Layout link, or drill into a specific record type and click the Homepage Layout link for the specific record type. This brings you to the Homepage Layout list, where you can edit an existing layout or create a new layout. Let us assume you are adding to an existing layout, since it is unlikely that you would be creating reports for a layout that does not yet exist.

Click the Edit link next to the layout for which you want to add the report. On the Homepage Layout Wizard screen, click the Step 2 Homepage Layout button or the Next button to get to the Homepage Layout screen shown in Figure 4-2.

The new homepage report will be listed in the Available Sections list. You may want to leave your homepage report here. Doing so includes the report as an option for users modifying their own homepage layouts. If you highlight the report in this list and move it left to the All Section list by clicking the < button between the All Section and Available Sections lists, the report will not be displayed on the homepage, nor will it be available for users to add to their personalized homepage.

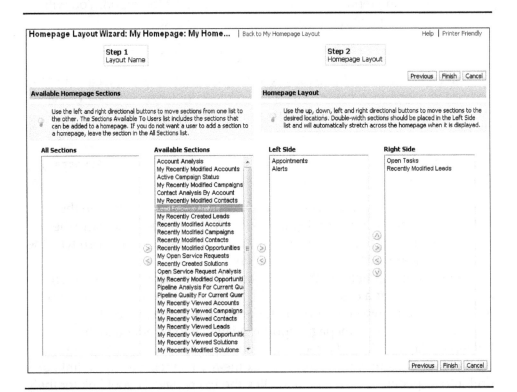

FIGURE 4-2.   *Homepage Layout Wizard*

If you move your report to one of the lists on the right side of this screen, the report will be displayed on the homepage. A single-width report will appear on the homepage in the column corresponding to the list in which you place it. A double-width report will span both columns, regardless of placement. Reports are also positioned on the homepage in the order listed within the Left Side or Right Side lists. Highlight the report and move it up and down in the list using the arrow buttons between the Left Side and Right Side lists.

Click Finish and your homepage layout is saved. Users who are already logged in when changes are made to the homepage layout will need to sign out and sign back in to Oracle CRM On Demand to see the changes.

Reports Inside Dashboards

Adding a report to a dashboard is something that I covered extensively in *Oracle CRM On Demand Dashboards* (McGraw-Hill/Professional, 2010), but I include it here as well simply because displaying a report in a dashboard is one of the many methods of embedding reports and I would be remiss if I did not give it some attention in this book as well. For a more complete description of dashboard development, please refer to my previous book. For a brief explanation of embedding reports inside of a dashboard, keep reading.

To add an existing report to a dashboard, navigate to the Dashboard tab and click the Manage Dashboards link. When you click the Manage Dashboards hyperlink on the Dashboard tab, you open the Manage Dashboards screen shown in Figure 4-3.

To the left of each dashboard name, you will find an Edit link along with a drop-down menu containing the Delete and Design links. Click the Design link to access the Dashboard Editor. It is on this screen, shown in Figure 4-4, that you add the report to the dashboard layout.

By clicking the Dashboard Name header, you can change the sort order of the dashboard list. Locate and drag the report you want to add to your dashboard from the Shared Content section to a section object on the dashboard layout. If you drop the report onto the layout outside of a section, the section object is automatically added to the dashboard as well as the report. In the Saved Content section, you will find the Shared Folders folder with the Company Wide Shared Folder and Pre-built Analysis folder within it. Clicking one of these folders expands the selected folder to expose the

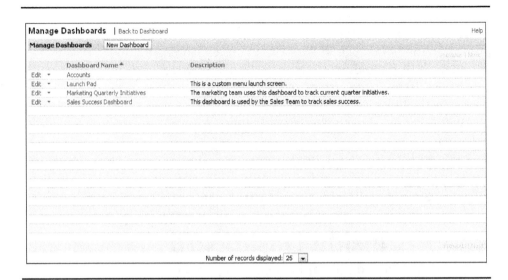

FIGURE 4-3. *Manage Dashboards screen*

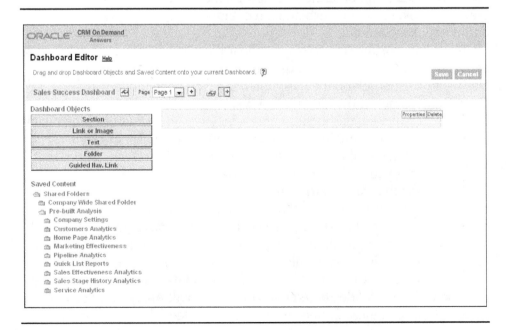

FIGURE 4-4. *Dashboard Editor*

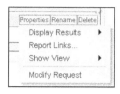

FIGURE 4-5.   *Report Object Properties menu*

subfolders and reports inside of it. Your My Folders folder is not included here in the Saved Content section. Personal reports are not permitted on dashboards.

Every report object on the dashboard layout has three buttons in the upper-right corner. The Properties button, the Rename button, and the Delete button are used to configure the report on the dashboard. Next I describe each of the configuration options in detail. We will start with the Properties menu. When you click Properties, you are presented with four options: Display Results, Report Links, Show View, and Modify Request. The Rename and Delete options are presented in their own buttons, and are also described next. Figure 4-5 shows the Properties menu opened on a report object in the Dashboard Editor screen.

Display Results

The first option in the Properties menu on the report object is actually a submenu with three options. There are three different ways to display a report in a dashboard. The default, and most common, method is to embed the report in the section so that the report displays as part of the dashboard. You can also set your reports to display as links that, when clicked, open the report in the dashboard window or in a separate window. When you click the Display Results item on the Properties menu, the Display Results submenu opens, as shown in Figure 4-6.

For a report embedded in the dashboard section, click the Properties button on the report object, and open the Display Results submenu. The Embedded In Section option is likely already selected, as this is the default, but if it is not, you should select it.

If you make no additional adjustments on the Properties menu described here, the report will display in its entirety. There are different strategies for

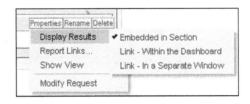

FIGURE 4-6. *Display Results submenu*

adjusting how reports display in the dashboard. The most common strategy, which I hope to change with the explanations in this book, is to duplicate a report that you want in your dashboard so that you have one version of the report that your users typically access from the Reports tab and another version, or many versions, of the report that include only the elements you want displayed in the dashboard. For instance, I often see companies with a report containing several views that they generally access via the Reports tab. This report will usually have a table, pivot table, and a couple of charts, along with a Title view. Now, if they want just the pivot table or just a chart on the dashboard, they replicate the same report and only include the desired view in the report. This is the report that is added to the dashboard. This is a valid method, and works perfectly well. Read on for some ideas on other strategies and their benefits.

The Link – Within The Dashboard option, which was mentioned in the previous chapter, displays a link to the report. Clicking the link in the dashboard replaces the contents of the dashboard window with the report results.

The Link – In A Separate Window option was also mentioned in the last chapter, and this option also displays a link to the report. Clicking this link in the dashboard opens a new window populated with the report results.

Report Links

There are three links that appear at the bottom of every report that you run from the Reports tab. You will always see the Refresh, Printer Friendly, and Download links at the end of your reports. You learned in the last chapter how to control the appearance of these links in a report by modifying the Go URL for the report. Reports displayed on a dashboard do not automatically

FIGURE 4-7.   *Report Links window*

include these three links at the base of the report. If you want any of these links on the individual report in the dashboard, you must enable them on the report object. Do this by clicking the Properties button and selecting the Report Links option. The Report Links window, shown in Figure 4-7, opens, displaying a check box for each of the report link options.

Clicking the Refresh check box on the Report Links window enables the Refresh link on the report within the dashboard. This will be a Refresh link at the bottom of the report in the dashboard in addition to the dashboard's Refresh link that appears at the bottom of the dashboard.

Clicking the report's Refresh link will resubmit the report query and the report will execute again within the dashboard. This is particularly useful when your dashboard includes real-time reports with data that changes frequently. Reports will often populate from cached data for increased performance. If the report has been executed recently, it may be cached. This cached version of the report could potentially contain stale data in an environment where data changes frequently. Clicking Refresh will run the report again, punching through the cache, so that the data in the report is current as of the moment run—assuming that the report is built on a Reporting subject area. A report built on one of the Analytics subject areas is pulling data from the data warehouse, which updates nightly, so clicking the Refresh link is not likely to cause any change in the data included in that report.

Clicking the Printer Friendly check box on the Report Links window enables the Printer Friendly link on the report within the dashboard. The Printer Friendly link will appear at the bottom of the report. The report Printer Friendly link is different from the Printer Friendly link that appears at the bottom of the dashboard. The dashboard Printer Friendly link operates the same as the report Printer Friendly link, in that it offers the same HTML and PDF options. The dashboard Printer Friendly link, however, opens the entire dashboard in a new browser window for printing.

Clicking the Download Link check box on the Report Links window enables the Download link on the report within the dashboard. The Download link will appear at the bottom of the report within the dashboard. The Download link, when clicked, offers a submenu with five download options.

Show View

With the choice of using dashboards to display reports, you have a number of options for how to set up your reports. The most common approach that I have seen among my customers is to create a separate report that is specifically for the dashboard. This could be a report developed just for the dashboard or a copy of another report that you strip down for the dashboard. Typically, when you add a report to a dashboard, the intent is to include just one view—a table or a chart. Most people will create a report and remove any unnecessary views, like the default Title and Table views.

What many dashboard developers do not realize is that copying and stripping down reports for dashboards is completely unnecessary because of the Show View option on the report object's Properties menu. When you click the Show View option in the Properties menu, you are presented with a submenu that contains a list of every view in the report. This list will include all views in the report, even views that you have removed from the active layout.

The Show View option allows you to select a single view to display in the dashboard. This means that you do not need to re-create a stripped-down version of a report in order to display only a single part of that report in the dashboard. This is great news for administrators who are concerned about the reports library becoming overrun with a lot of reports. This is even better news for the report developer, who can accomplish many things and fill multiple requirements with a single report.

The default selection in the Show View menu is Default Compound View. The Default Compound View selection indicates that all visible views in the report should be included in the dashboard. In other words, the report appears in the dashboard exactly as it would if you ran the report from the

Reports tab. Because all reports have a Title view and Table view by default, the Show View menu will also always contain the Title 1 and Table 1 options in addition to Default Compound View. Because the Show View menu will also contain all of the views that have been added to a report, even if they were subsequently removed, it is possible for a report to appear one way when run from the Reports tab and display a view that does not appear in the report on a dashboard.

Modify Request

The final option on the Properties menu is Modify Request. Clicking Modify Request takes you out of the Dashboard Editor to the Build And View Analysis screen. The report from the dashboard is opened in the editor, ready for you to make modifications. This is a nice shortcut to Answers On Demand for editing your reports. The Build And View Analysis screen opens up on the Define Criteria step. Here you can modify the columns, filters, and column formats. Moving to step 2 permits you to modify and add views in the report.

Rename

Clicking the Rename button on the report object in the dashboard opens a small Rename window, as shown in Figure 4-8. The name of the report is the default value in this screen, but you can overwrite that name here. The name of the report as listed here only appears on the Dashboard Editor window, unless you have added the report as a link and have selected the Use Dashboard Object Name As Link Text check box. With this check box selected, the text you enter on the Rename window will appear as the linked text on the dashboard. This text does not affect the link target in any way.

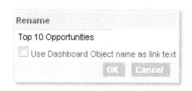

FIGURE 4-8.   *Rename window*

Delete

Wrapping up our tour of the report object on the dashboard, we have the Delete button. Its function is obvious. If you click the Delete button on the report, the entire report is removed from the dashboard layout. Clicking Delete does not delete the report from Oracle CRM On Demand. It simply removes the report from the dashboard.

Using Inline Frames to Embed Reports

In the last chapter, you saw the Go URL used for linking to reports by inserting the URL inside of an HTML anchor tag. When embedding a report, you will do something very similar, except we will be using the HTML inline frame (iFrame) tag rather than the anchor tag. This method is used in most of the remaining methods for embedding reports described in this chapter.

I included a little bit about the iFrame tag in Chapter 1. I will review some of that information here, but the thing you really need to know about the iFrame is that it creates an HTML window (or frame) on the screen, and the screen, in our case, is a report or a web applet. We can display another webpage inside of that inline frame by referencing the page's URL as the source within the iFrame. When that URL references a report, you will display the target report inside of the inline frame. If you add a narrative view to a report and then place an iFrame inside the narrative view, you have just embedded one report inside of another. More on that later—for now, let us review the inline frame HTML tags.

The syntax for an inline frame, like most HTML tags, requires an open and a close tag. Your iFrame will begin with <IFRAME ...> and will end with </IFRAME>. Each inline frame needs a source URL. That source URL is the specific webpage that you want to display within the frame. For instance, if you wanted to display the Oracle website inside of an inline frame, your HTML would look something like this:

```
<IFRAME SRC=http://www.oracle.com></IFRAME>
```

Of course, it would be rather unusual for a webpage to fit neatly inside of an inline frame, since the default size of the frame is 300 pixels wide and

150 pixels high. The height and width attributes allow you to control the size of the frame. This is very important when embedding reports inside of web applets and other reports. The following HTML would embed the Oracle webpage inside of a frame that is 800 pixels wide by 600 pixels high:

```
<IFRAME SRC=http://www.oracle.com HEIGHT=600 WIDTH=800></IFRAME>
```

You can also use a relative size value in these attributes. For instance, if you want to restrict the height of the frame but allow the frame to grow to fit the full width of your screen, the HTML would look something like this:

```
<IFRAME SRC=http://www.oracle.com HEIGHT=600 WIDTH="100%"></IFRAME>
```

I also find that the default border around the inline frame tends to make my embedded reports look like they have been pasted on top of the page rather than actually embedded as part of the page, so I like to take the border off. Also, if I have set the size of the frame properly, the scroll bars will not appear within the frame, but just to be sure, you can turn off the scroll bars.

```
<IFRAME SRC=http://www.oracle.com HEIGHT=600 WIDTH="100%"
FRAMEBORDER=0 SCROLLING=no></IFRAME>
```

So, by combining the inline frame tag with a Go URL for a report, it is possible to embed reports inside of an iFrame, and iFrames may be used in a variety of places within Oracle CRM On Demand, allowing you to embed reports and other webpages throughout the application.

Embedding Reports Inside Reports

In this section I describe the process of embedding one report inside of another report. The first obvious question to answer here is why we would want to embed one report inside of another. At one time, this was the work-around method for creating custom dashboards before Oracle CRM On Demand provided custom dashboard functionality. Since the addition of custom dashboards, I do this much less than before, but there are still some circumstances where I use this method of embedding reports. One that came up recently for me was a need to include more than one hundred columns in a report. Reports in Oracle CRM On Demand do not allow that many columns, so my solution was to embed multiple reports into another report and link them up using a filter identified in the Go URL for the embedded report. I have also used this method as an alternative to a combined analysis when I needed to report on two different record types that were not available in the same subject area but were related by some intermediary record—opportunities and service requests related to a particular account, for instance. The Opportunity report is easy, as is the Service Request report, but a single report that shows both sets of data is a bit trickier.

To embed one report inside of another, you will use a narrative view in the host report and the Go URL of the embedded report to display the embedded report inside that narrative view. A narrative view accepts HTML, so naturally, we will use an inline frame with a report URL as its source to bring in the report. If you examine the sample report in Figure 4-9, it is not readily apparent that the Contact List portion of this report is actually a separate report embedded inside of the main report.

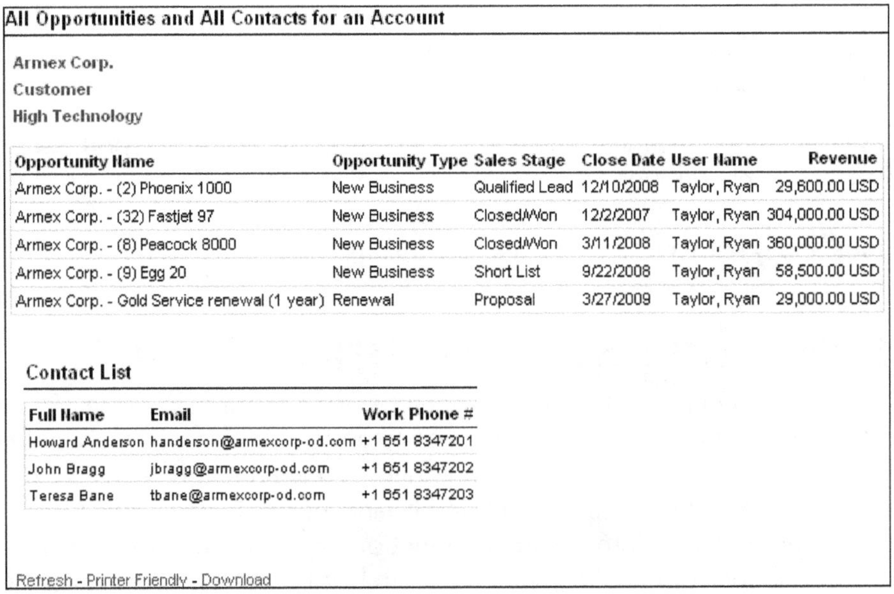

All Opportunities and All Contacts for an Account					

Armex Corp.
Customer
High Technology

Opportunity Name	Opportunity Type	Sales Stage	Close Date	User Name	Revenue
Armex Corp. - (2) Phoenix 1000	New Business	Qualified Lead	12/10/2008	Taylor, Ryan	29,600.00 USD
Armex Corp. - (32) Fastjet 97	New Business	Closed/Won	12/2/2007	Taylor, Ryan	304,000.00 USD
Armex Corp. - (8) Peacock 8000	New Business	Closed/Won	3/11/2008	Taylor, Ryan	360,000.00 USD
Armex Corp. - (9) Egg 20	New Business	Short List	9/22/2008	Taylor, Ryan	58,500.00 USD
Armex Corp. - Gold Service renewal (1 year)	Renewal	Proposal	3/27/2009	Taylor, Ryan	29,000.00 USD

Contact List

Full Name	Email	Work Phone #
Howard Anderson	handerson@armexcorp-od.com	+1 651 8347201
John Bragg	jbragg@armexcorp-od.com	+1 651 8347202
Teresa Bane	tbane@armexcorp-od.com	+1 651 8347203

Refresh - Printer Friendly - Download

FIGURE 4-9. *Report embedded inside another report*

| Title | | | | | | ⁴⁄₄ ⦹ × |

All Opportunities and All Contacts for an Account

| Pivot Table | | | | | | ⁴⁄₄ ⦹ × |

Armex Corp.
Customer
High Technology

Opportunity Name	Opportunity Type	Sales Stage	Close Date	User Name	Revenue
Armex Corp. - (2) Phoenix 1000	New Business	Qualified Lead	12/10/2008	Taylor, Ryan	29,600.00 USD
Armex Corp. - (32) Fastjet 97	New Business	Closed/Won	12/2/2007	Taylor, Ryan	304,000.00 USD
Armex Corp. - (8) Peacock 8000	New Business	Closed/Won	3/11/2008	Taylor, Ryan	360,000.00 USD
Armex Corp. - (9) Egg 20	New Business	Short List	9/22/2008	Taylor, Ryan	58,500.00 USD
Armex Corp. - Gold Service renewal (1 year)	Renewal	Proposal	3/27/2009	Taylor, Ryan	29,000.00 USD

| Narrative | | | | | | ⁴⁄₄ ⦹ × |

Contact List

Full Name	Email	Work Phone #
Howard Anderson	handerson@armexcorp-od.com	+1 651 8347201
John Bragg	jbragg@armexcorp-od.com	+1 651 8347202
Teresa Bane	tbane@armexcorp-od.com	+1 651 8347203

FIGURE 4-10. *Report embedded inside another report – Create Layout view*

Now, examine Figure 4-10. This is the Create Layout view of the same report. Notice that a pivot table is responsible for the list of opportunities associated with the selected account and that the contact list appears inside of a narrative view.

In Figure 4-11, I am showing you the HTML that is inside the narrative view. Notice that the Narrative field contains the iFrame tag with a source URL that points to a report named ContactList. This is the embedded report. Also, notice that the Options attribute in the report URL has no values. This suppresses the Refresh, Printer Friendly, and Download links in the embedded report.

It is usually important in this type of report that the embedded report be filtered using data from the main report. Generally, when you are embedding one report inside of another, there is some common element in both reports.

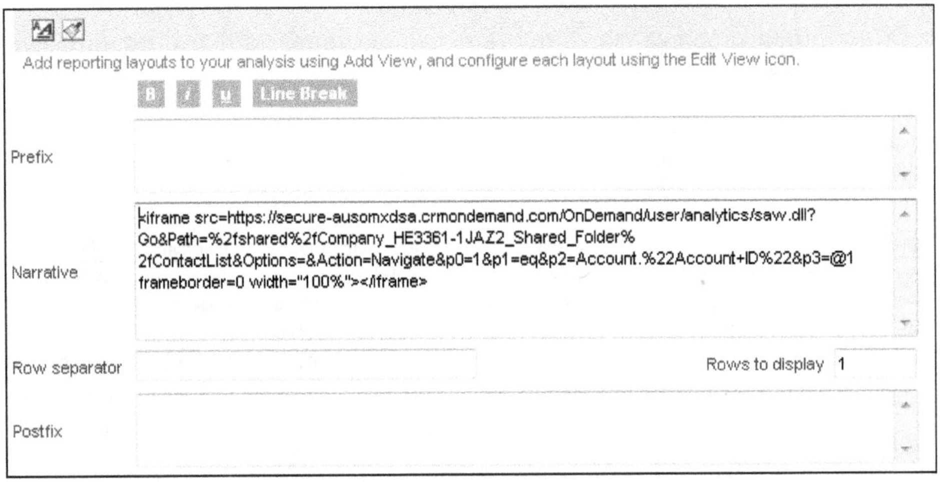

Add reporting layouts to your analysis using Add View, and configure each layout using the Edit View icon.

B **i** **u** **Line Break**

Prefix

Narrative
```
<iframe src=https://secure-ausomxdsa.crmondemand.com/OnDemand/user/analytics/saw.dll?
Go&Path=%2fshared%2fCompany_HE3361-1JAZ2_Shared_Folder%
2fContactList&Options=&Action=Navigate&p0=1&p1=eq&p2=Account.%22Account+ID%22&p3=@1
frameborder=0 width="100%"></iframe>
```

Row separator   Rows to display 1

Postfix

FIGURE 4-11. *Narrative view*

In this case, it is the account. The main report shows a list of all opportunities associated with the account, and the embedded report lists all of the contacts associated with the same account. So we need to include this filter in our URL for the embedded report. The filter attributes in the Go URL are the same as those we saw in the previous chapter, but you will notice that the value in the p3 attribute is set to @1 rather than a specific value.

In a narrative view, the nomenclature used to reference columns within the report is @n, where n is the column number. In this case, @1 refers to the first column in the report, which is the Account ID column. The contents of the Narrative field within the narrative view will appear something like this:

```
<iframe src=https://secure-ausomxdsa.crmondemand.com/OnDemand/user/
analytics/saw.dll?Go&Path=%2fshared%2fCompany_HI2337-1OSS0_Shared_
Folder%2fContactList&Options=&Action=Navigate&p0=1&p1=eq&p2=
Account.%22Account+ID%22&p3=@1 frameborder=0 width="100%"></iframe>
```

Of course, it is not required to link the embedded report with the data from the main report. If you do not need to filter the embedded report, you do not need to include the filter attributes in your report URL.

Embedding Dashboards Inside Reports

Okay, so at this point it may seem like embedding a dashboard inside of a report is just showing off, but there really is a benefit to doing this. I have done this many times for my customers. Have you ever noticed that some of the pre-built reports in Oracle CRM On Demand have prompts presented across the top of the report? This style of prompt is something you may have developed for a dashboard before, but there is no way to add such prompts to your custom reports without the use of a dashboard. Since you cannot overwrite the pre-built reports, it is not possible to simply make a change to one of these reports and replace it with a new version. In fact, if you edit a pre-built report, the filter prompts are lost entirely from the report.

This describes one source of frustration for many customers, who find that a pre-built report is perfect for their business, except for one or two columns. Others simply want to be able to set all of their filter values on a single screen.

Of course, it would be perfectly acceptable for most to just build a dashboard with the report and dashboard filter, and have users access the dashboard on the Dashboard tab. In fact, you absolutely must build a dashboard with the dashboard filter prompt and report in order to present both on the same screen. However, not all of my customers are keen on sending users to the Dashboard tab for some reports and the Reports tab for other reports. So, when my customer tells me that they want a report listed on the Reports tab that contains a dashboard filter prompt, I have to get creative.

This book does not describe building dashboards and dashboard filter prompts in detail, but you can refer to *Oracle CRM On Demand Dashboards* (McGraw-Hill/Professional, 2010) for that information. Earlier in this chapter I described embedding a report inside of a dashboard, and in the previous chapter, I described the process for locating the dashboard URL. Next is the simple matter of building a report that contains an embedded dashboard.

We need a report to host the dashboard. Usually, when I embed a dashboard inside of a report, the report that I am using to host the dashboard is really nothing more than a blank page. In other words, what I really need is a report with no columns in it—an empty webpage of sorts. Every report in Oracle CRM On Demand has to reference at least one column from the database, so an absolutely blank report is not really possible. What I normally do here is create a report that contains a single metric column. I always select an Analytics subject area for performance, something like the Account History subject area and the # of Accounts column. I try to select the record type with the fewest number of records in it, again for performance. Other than performance, the choice of subject area is of no consequence. I recommend a single metric column so that the result will return only a single record with a single row. Next, format the column as hidden. Do this by clicking the Column Properties button, moving to the Column Format tab, and selecting the Hide This Column check box.

On the report layout, remove the Title view and Table view. Now we have a blank webpage to work with. Add a narrative view to the report. Just like embedding a report inside of a report, we will use a narrative view with an inline frame to bring on the dashboard. The Narrative field of your narrative view will contain the HTML code with the iFrame tag. The inline frame will contain the dashboard URL as the source. A sample of this code is shown here followed by a sample report containing a dashboard in Figure 4-12:

```
<iframe src=https://secure-ausomxbwa.crmondemand.com/OnDemand/user/
analytics/saw.dll?Dashboard&PortalPath=%2fshared%2fCompany_12345_
Shared_Folder%2f_portal%2fOpportunity+Dashboard width="100%"
height=500 frameborder=0 scrolling=no></iframe>
```

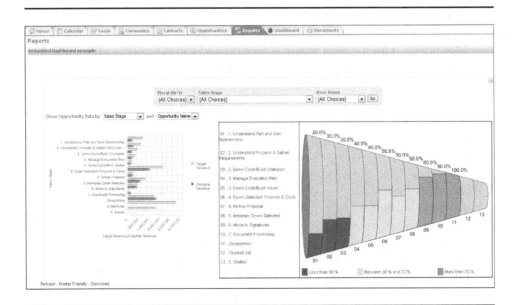

FIGURE 4-12. *Report with embedded dashboard*

Embedding Reports Inside Applets

Suppose you want to display some specific information, perhaps a chart, on a record detail page. You want this information to be specifically related to the current record that you are displaying on the screen. The solution is to embed your report into a custom Web applet and add the applet to your homepage.

The first step is to build the report that you want to embed into your web applet. This report should contain just the views that you wish to display within the applet. I usually remove the Title view and try to limit the report to a single view, usually a table, pivot table, or chart. When I build a report for embedding, I think about how I want that report to appear on the screen in context with the rest of the screen. Essentially, I try to make the report appear less like a report and more like the other elements of the screen. The more natural the embedded report looks in its environment, the more users tend to accept the report and think of it as just another element of the application rather than a report.

There are two types of web applets in Oracle CRM On Demand. They are essentially the same, but the global web applet can be included on the Home tab and in the Action bar. The record type-specific web applets can be included on the homepage or detail page of the specific record type. To create a web applet, click the Admin Global link to access the Admin homepage, and then click the Application Customization link to open the Application Customization screen. From here, you can click the Global Web Applets link or drill into a specific record type and click the Web Applet link within the specific record type.

This brings you to a list of web applets, which will be blank if you have not previously created any web applets. Clicking the Edit link next to an existing web applet or clicking the New button on this screen will bring you to the Custom Web Applet edit screen shown in Figure 4-13.

On this screen, you will need to give your web applet a name, and then specify the location for the applet. Your options here vary, depending on the type of web applet you are creating. For a record-specific applet, you can choose between Homepage and Detail Page. For a global web applet, you can choose between Homepage and Action Bar.

If you select Homepage in the Location field, you will also need to select the column width in the Columns field. Selecting Single creates a web applet that spans a single column. The Double option spans your web applet across both columns on your homepage.

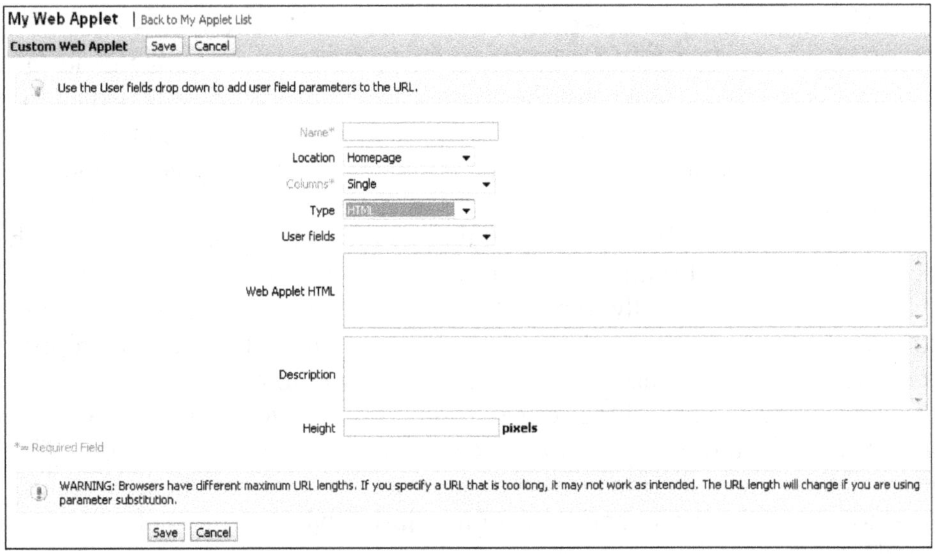

FIGURE 4-13. *Custom Web Applet edit screen*

For embedding reports, I select the HTML option in the Type field. Technically, you can embed a report using just the URL, but using HTML with an iFrame, you have a little more control over the display of the report within the applet.

Depending on the type of web applet you are creating, you will have one or two drop-down list fields that allow you to select user fields or record-specific fields to insert into the code for the web applet. For instance, selecting Opportunity Id from the Opportunity Fields list when creating an opportunity web applet inserts %%%Id%%% into the Web Applet HTML field. This nomenclature should be familiar if you have created a web link for accessing a report as described in the last chapter. We use these field references in the Go URL for the report as shown in the following Web Applet HTML code:

```
<iframe src=/OnDemand/user/analytics/saw.dll?Go&Path=
%2fshared%2fCompany_00000_Shared_Folder%2fProduct+Applet&Options=
r&Action=Navigate&p0=1&p1=eq&p2=Opportunity."Opportunity+ID"&p3=
%%%Id%%% FRAMEBORDER="no" WIDTH="100%" HEIGHT=300></iframe>
```

Once you have your web applet HTML set up to insert the intended report into the applet, you will save the web applet and return to the Web Applet list. Next up is exposing the web applet on the homepage, detail screen, or Action bar. Do this from the Application Customization screen by drilling onto the desired layout configuration and adding the applet to the list of visible elements.

Embedding Reports and Dashboards on a Web Tab

Custom web tabs are great for making a frequently referenced report or dashboard easy to access and use. When you create a custom web tab in Oracle CRM On Demand, you are asked for the URL for the site that you wish to display within the tab. To display a report or dashboard here, you simply provide the URL.

To create a new web tab, click the Admin Global link to get to the Admin homepage, and click Application Customization. From the Application Customization screen, click the Custom Web Tab link to access the Custom Web Tab list. On this screen you can edit existing tabs or click the New button to create a new web tab.

You will create or edit your web tab on the Custom Web Tab screen (Figure 4-14). The name you provide in the Name field will be the tab name that appears in Oracle CRM On Demand. Enter the report or dashboard URL into the URL field. No inline frame tags are needed here. In fact, configuring a custom web tab is like using a wizard to create an HTML inline frame. Notice the Frame Height and Frame Width fields. Enter your desired frame size here in pixels, just like you would if configuring an inline frame.

If your report is filtered for the current user or on some other user field, you can use the User Fields list to select and insert the field variable into your URL. The description is only visible on the Web Tab list and does not appear on the web tab itself.

Tabs in Oracle CRM On Demand all contain an icon to the left of the tab name. A custom web tab is not different, and you can select an icon for your web tab by clicking the Lookup button on the Icon field. This opens the icon library window (Figure 4-15), allowing you to click on the icon you want to display on your custom web tab.

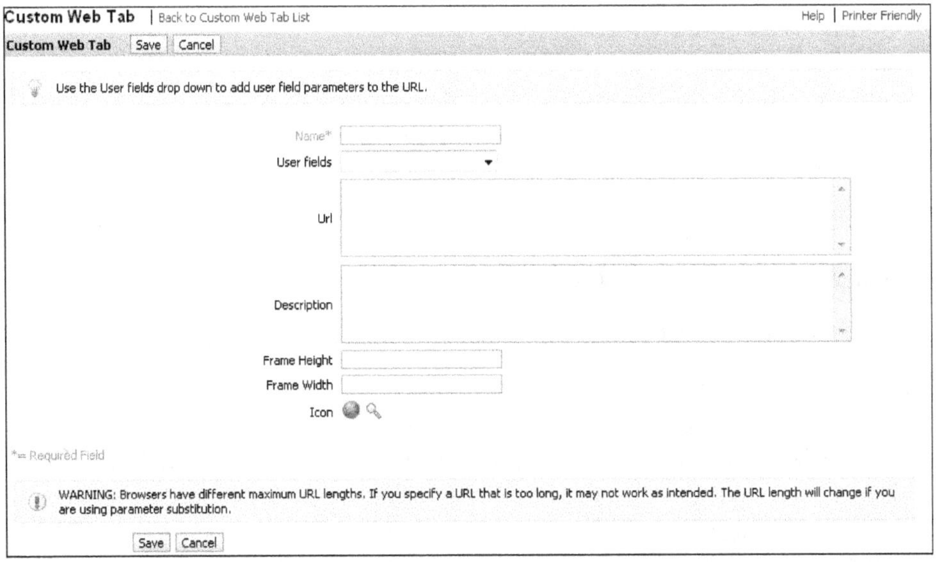

FIGURE 4-14. *Custom Web Tab window*

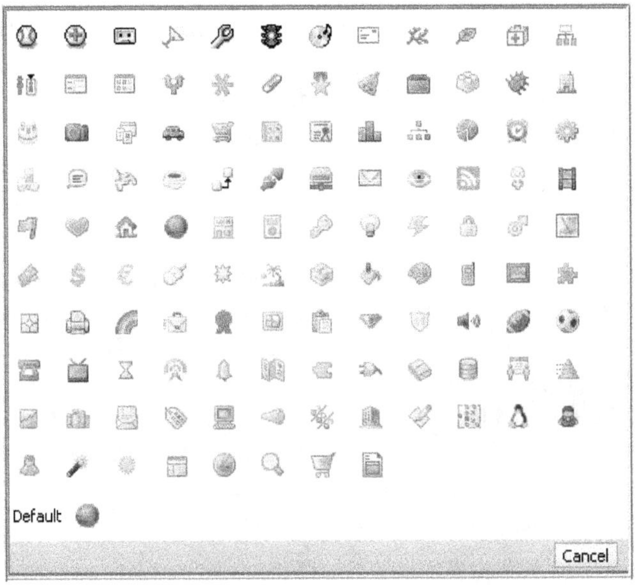

FIGURE 4-15. *Tab icon library window*

Web tabs, like web applets, need to be exposed in order to be visible to your users. Web tabs are a bit different, however, in that you are not adding them to a layout or homepage. Access to web tabs is role-based. In order for a user to have access to a web tab, the tab must be included as one of the available or selected tabs in the user's role. Access to tabs is provided on the Step 5 Tab Access & Order screen within the Role Management Wizard. If you do not have access to role management, ask your system administrator for help. The basic process for adding an existing web tab to a role is provided in Table 4-1.

Now that we have covered the process for embedding a report or dashboard on a custom web tab, let's review a few interesting uses for reports and dashboards embedded in a web tab. I use this technique often, and it seems to be a popular use of the custom web tab.

---

1. Click the Admin global link.

2. Click the User Management And Access Controls link.

3. Click the Role Management link.

4. Click the Edit link next to the role to which you want to provide web tab access.

5. Click Step 5 Tab Access & Order.

6. Locate the web tab in the Not Available Tab list, and click it.

7. Click the > button located between the Not Available Tab list and Available Tabs list. This makes the tab available to users with this role, but does not automatically display the tab.

8. With the tab highlighted in the Available Tabs list, click the > button between the Available Tabs list and the Selected Tabs list. This adds the tab to the visible tabs for the role.

9. Position the tab by using the up and down arrows located to the right of the Selected Tabs list. The tab listed at the top of the list is the leftmost tab on the Oracle CRM On Demand screens.

10. Click the Finish button.

TABLE 4-1. *Steps to Add a Web Tab to a Role*

Custom Home Tab

A custom web tab positioned at the top of the Selected Tabs list in the Role Settings area will be the first tab in Oracle CRM On Demand, and will, therefore, be the tab that users will see as soon as they sign in to the application. This is a great opportunity to push analytical and report data to the user's screen, and many companies have used this tactic to deliver some business-critical and often time-dependant information to the users every time they sign on to Oracle CRM On Demand.

Critical service requests, hot sales leads, past due activities, and many other bits of information can be presented on the custom web tab using an embedded dashboard. If you have just one or two small reports, those can be added to the standard Home tab as homepage reports. With a dashboard embedded on a web tab, you can present multiple reports. Those reports can contain hyperlinks to other reports and records.

Reports presented on the custom homepage web tab can be automatically filtered based on the current user, and can be different for each role since the web tabs are assigned to specific roles. I even know of one company that took this concept to an extreme and practically replaced the Oracle CRM On Demand user interface with dashboards and custom web tabs. This would not be practical for many, but does demonstrate the possibilities of embedding reports and dashboards.

Custom Report Menu

Another common use of the custom web tab with an embedded report is the custom report menu. I have done this for many of my customers, particularly those who have a large number of reports. To ease confusion and alleviate the hassle of maintaining a lot of report folder security settings, many companies create a custom web tab for each role that serves as a custom menu report. Using the techniques described in the previous chapter for creating report hyperlinks inside of a narrative view on a report, it is quite easy to develop a page of links that can be arranged any way you like. This report with the hyperlinks is then embedded in a custom web tab. Now, users with access to that report menu custom web tab simply open the tab in Oracle CRM On Demand, and all of the links to the reports they need are on the screen, ready to use. The links can be set to open the report in the same screen or in a new window. I have sometimes even used clickable images on the screen. You could even get creative with this and create a screen full of buttons that target different reports, dashboards, or even other screens within Oracle CRM On Demand.

Role-Based Dashboard Access

Dashboards in Oracle CRM On Demand are a fantastic way to deliver reports and analytical information to your users. One issue that I have heard from many of my customers is that access to dashboards is "all or nothing." In other words, your users either have access to the Dashboard tab or they do not, and if they have access to dashboards, they see all of the dashboards in the list of dashboards on the tab.

If you want to relieve your users of these dashboards that they will never need or use, the only way to do this is to give them a new place to find their dashboard. This new place is a custom web tab with their dashboard embedded on the screen. There are a couple of benefits to delivering dashboards in this way. Users do not have to sort through a list of dashboards to find the one they want. Running the dashboard requires a single click of the custom web tab rather than the four clicks it takes to click the Dashboard tab, open the dashboard list, select the dashboard from the list, and click the Show button. Finally, the custom web tab can be exposed to show only the roles that need the dashboard, giving users a unique and appropriate user experience.

Bear in mind that with all of these custom web tab deliveries of dashboards and reports, users still need access to dashboards and reports. You are not bypassing those access controls by embedding reports and dashboards. The Dashboard tab and Reports tab do not have to be one of the selected tabs for the user's role, but access to them must be available.

Custom Search Tab

One of the most often requested dashboards that I build for my customers is a custom search tool. With a well-designed dashboard filter prompt, it is quite easy to provide your users with a sophisticated search tool. One thing that it is possible to do with a dashboard-based search that is not possible with the standard search function in Oracle CRM On Demand is a keyword search that is applied to multiple columns at once. This is achieved using the presentation variables. For more information on building dashboards, please refer to *Oracle CRM On Demand Dashboards* (McGraw-Hill/ Professional, 2010).

Every time I build a custom search dashboard, I embed it onto a custom web tab. The search results usually contain hyperlinks to the records in the search results.

Report Widget

So far, we have discussed embedding reports in screens all over Oracle CRM On Demand, but what if you want to access a report outside of Oracle CRM On Demand? Well, there is a way to embed reports and dashboards into desktop applications that support widgets, portals, or in a stand-alone webpage. The HTML code that you need to perform such a task is actually generated for you within the application, making this process that much easier.

I should point out that anyone accessing an Oracle CRM On Demand screen, including reports and dashboards, must have a user sign-on ID and password. The widget will request an ID and password before displaying any reports, dashboards, or lists. It is also important to note that the feature described here is only available if your system administrator has enabled the privileges on your role. The Embed CRM On Demand Widgets privilege gives you permission to access Oracle CRM On Demand content outside of the application. Without this privilege, your login will fail when attempted through a widget. The Manage Custom Web Applets privilege gives you permission to create, edit, and publish custom widgets.

Oracle CRM On Demand allows four different types of widgets, as you can see in Figure 4-16. This figure shows the Embed CRM On Demand Content screen. Access this screen by clicking the My Setup global link, and then click the Embed CRM On Demand Content link in the Data & Integrations Tools section of your Personal Homepage screen.

On this screen, Oracle CRM On Demand provides you with the necessary HTML code for embedding a widget in other applications. When you add this HTML to an external application and run that application, you first see an Oracle CRM On Demand login window. Once you have provided a valid ID and password, the widget content appears.

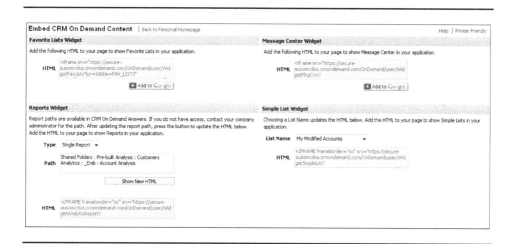

FIGURE 4-16. *Embed CRM On Demand Content screen*

Four widgets are available:

- The **Favorite Lists Widget** displays your favorite Oracle CRM On Demand lists. Typically, your favorite lists applet appears on the Action bar in Oracle CRM On Demand, but this widget makes that applet available outside of the CRM application. You can copy the HTML code provided to add the widget to your application, or click the Add To Google button to add the widget to your iGoogle page, if you are using that service.

- The **Message Center Widget** allows you to access messages received in the Message Center of Oracle CRM On Demand without requiring you to first open Oracle CRM On Demand. The Message Center is generally located in the Action bar. You can copy the HTML code provided to add the widget to your application, or click the Add To Google button to add the widget to your iGoogle page.

- The **Simple List Widget** allows you to select one of the "My Modified" record lists and then provides the HTML code necessary to embed that list into your external application. This simple widget displays a single list of record names, each hyperlinked to the appropriate detail screen in Oracle CRM On Demand.

■ The **Reports Widget** displays a report created in Oracle CRM On Demand in your external application. To create a widget that contains a dashboard or report, you first select either Single Report or Dashboard in the Type field. In the Path field, you will enter the path to the report. The path to a report should be entered in the following syntax:

```
Company Wide Shared Folder : <Folder Name> : <Report Name>
```

This is exactly the same report path syntax we use when creating a homepage report. After entering the path, click the Show New HTML button to update the HTML code in the HTML field. This is the code you will copy and paste into your external application to create the widget. For example, a report named Widget Chart saved in the Company Wide Shared Folder has the following path:

```
Company Wide Shared Folder : Widget Chart
```

The HTML code that this generates is shown here:

```
<IFRAME frameborder="no" src="https://secure-
ausomxdsa.crmondemand.com/OnDemand/user/WidgetAnalyticReport?lpr=
1&AnalyticWidget.Path=
Company+Wide+Shared+Folder+%3a+Widget+Chart&AnalyticWidget.Type=
Single+Report" scrolling="auto" id="On Demand Widget" onload=
"this.style.height='500px';this.style.width=
'350px';window.scrollTo(0,0);">Browser does not support IFRAMES.</
IFRAME>
```

You will notice that this is not the standard Go URL for reports that we have used for linking and embedding reports inside of Oracle CRM On Demand. Most of this code needs to remain exactly as shown, but I have found that it is possible to tweak the height and width and turn off the scrolling. These elements are part of the inline frame code and do not affect the report.

I would like to also point out here that I have indeed tried embedding the code for these widgets inside of a narrative view in a report, and yes, it does actually work. That being said, I cannot think of a compelling reason to embed a widget inside of a report, and have never had a customer make a request that compelled me to do so.

External Sites Embedded Inside Reports

One request I get from sales folks quite often is to embed some external site into Oracle CRM On Demand, and this often involves some sort of report. The most popular example of this is a map embedded into the application that plots customer addresses. Google is probably the most popular map site for doing this sort of mash-up into other applications. This may be because Google freely provides their application programming interface (API) code for developers to integrate Google applications into their programs.

To date, I have used the Google version 2 API within Oracle CRM On Demand. As of this writing, the version 2 API is being deprecated in favor of a new version, but version 2 is still supported. If you or someone you know is skilled with JavaScript, you should have no problems using either version to embed a map into your report. Next, I describe the high-level process of embedding a Google map that plots multiple addresses inside of a report.

Begin by developing a report that contains the addresses you want to plot on the map. To this report you will add the narrative view to host the Google API code. There would be no benefit to including the specific code here for you, since your usage and your report will certainly be different from mine, and you certainly do not want to try to retype this code into your narrative view. Copy and paste it from the Google sites, but do have a look at Figure 4-17, where I show a sample narrative view containing the Google Map API code.

You see in the screen shot that there are lines of code in the Prefix field, Narrative field, and Postfix field. The difference between these three fields in the narrative view is that the Prefix and Postfix content appears once in the view and is not tied to the records returned by the report. A report that returns 20 rows and a report that returns a single row will treat the prefix and postfix code exactly the same. The content in the Narrative field is repeated for each row, and it is here that you insert fields from the report into the content of the narrative report. In code such as the Google Maps API, the Prefix and Postfix fields contain the JavaScript code that generates the Google map. The portion of the code that performs the reverse geocoding of the addresses and populates the pop-up information bubbles, as shown in Figure 4-18, is entered into the Narrative field. The content of the Narrative field is tied to the records returned in the report, so a report that returns 20 rows will repeat the contents of the Narrative field 20 times.

Add reporting layouts to your analysis using Add View, and configure each layout using the Edit View icon.

> **B** *I* **U** **Line Break**

Prefix
```
<script src="http://maps.google.com/maps?
file=api&amp;v=2&amp;sensor=false&amp;key=ABQIAAAAfjTUS1rwjZFFLcR-
PuFhKxTB8oHeFj7CBa41Cy5QnqMBRUvuXBSXPTEjuICsav57hNRcVblBBrfxDA "
```

Narrative
```
showAddress('@3, @4, @5', '<a href=/OnDemand/user/AccountDetail?
OMTGT=AccountDetailForm&AccountDetailForm.Id=@11 target="_top">@1</a> [br/]@9  @10[br/]
Annual Revenue of @8');
```

Row separator _____   Rows to display _____

Postfix
```
}
</script>
<script src="http://code.jquery.com/jquery-latest.js" type="text/javascript"></script>
    <script type="text/javascript">
```

FIGURE 4-17. *Narrative view with Google Map API code*

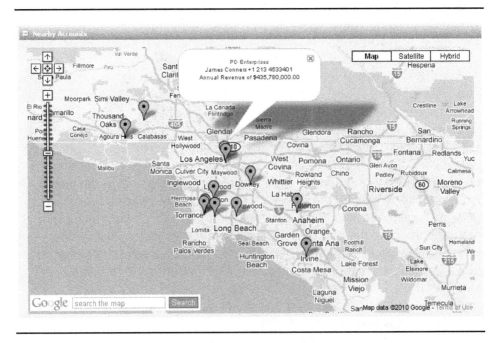

FIGURE 4-18. *Sample Google Map embedded in a report*

Let us examine this portion of the code a little more carefully, since it is where our code will differ from what you copy off of Google's website.

```
showAddress('@3, @4, @5', '<a href=/OnDemand/user/
AccountDetail?OMTGT=AccountDetailForm&AccountDetailForm.Id=@11
target="_top">@1</a> [br/]@9 @10[br/]Annual Revenue of @8');
```

The showAddress command of the Google code is repeated for every address in the map. Since we are mapping multiple addresses and pulling in address values from our report, it makes perfect sense that this line of code would fall into the Narrative field. The showAddress command needs a street address, city, and state to locate an address on the map. These three columns are the third, fourth, and fifth columns in my report, so the first three values inside the showAddress command are @3, @4, and @5. The fourth value provides the content of the pop-up window on the address marker. As you see in Figure 4-18, I am including the company name, primary contact, primary contact phone number, and the company annual revenue in my information bubble. These are also values in my report. Column one (@1) is my company name, Columns nine and ten (@9 and @10) contain the contact name and phone number. Annual revenue is in column eight (@8). You will notice that I include some additional HTML code here to insert page breaks, and I have also included an anchor tag to generate a hyperlink to the account detail screen for each company. For this link I need the account ID, so I added that column to my report in the eleventh column (@11) so I could include it here in my hyperlink.

This report with content from an external site embedded can now be used like any other report in Oracle CRM On Demand. Users can run it from the Reports tab, see it embedded in a dashboard, see it embedded in a web applet or web tab, or link into it from another screen. And this is just one example of embedding external content. The current trends in social media and the sharing of content across different web spaces opens up many possibilities for embedding external content into Oracle CRM On Demand. When you need to use data from Oracle CRM On Demand in your mash-up with external content, reports are a natural environment for hosting your embedded content.

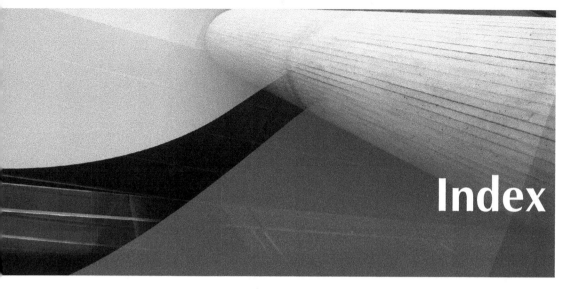

Index

A

<A> tags, 20
Abbreviate option, 48
Access All Data privilege, 9
Access All Data in Analytics privilege, 4
Access Analytics Dashboards
    privilege, 4
Access Analytics Reports privilege, 4
Access Analytics Reports - View Prebuilt
    Reports privilege, 4
access controls
    administrator, 5–7
    report developers, 3–5
Account Detail screen, 108
Account Edit screen, 114
Account records
    ActionLinks, 107
    text format links, 110
Action bar, applets on, 147–149
Action tags
    dashboard links, 123–124
    description, 89
    Go URLs, 93–94
    URLs, 91
ActionLinks
    description, 12
    working with, 105–107
Active Filters view, 39

Add Navigation Target button, 99
Add Target Report button, 102
Add View menu, 45
Additional Charting Options window
    for navigation, 101–102
    pivot charts, 83
    settings, 50–52
Additional Gauge Properties window,
    62–63
Address (URL) field, 90
Admin homepage, 130, 149
administrator access controls, 5–7
Advanced Options window
    charts, 50
    Gauge view, 62
After option for pivot tables, 74, 78, 80
aggregation
    column data, 43
    pivot tables, 77
alignment
    in cells, 31
    report views, 41
    tables, 42
    text, 72
All Choices hyperlink, 37–38
Analytics Scripting privilege, 5
anchor tags, 20, 103
AND connectors for filters, 38
Appearance tab for Gauge view, 62

applets, embedding inside reports,
147–149
Application Customization screen,
130–131, 147, 149
Apply Saved Filter window, 38–39
Appointment records, 110
area charts, 54–55
Asset records, 110
At The Beginning option for pivot tables,
68, 74, 78, 80
At The End option for pivot tables,
74, 78, 80
attributes in HTML, 16
Axis Limits settings, 48–49
Axis Scaling window
pivot charts, 83
settings, 48–49
Axis Titles & Labels window
pivot charts, 82
settings, 47

Borders & Colors tab
charts, 51–52
Gauge view, 61
Bottom tab for charts, 48, 83
bottom value in Go URLs, 97

 tags, 18
breakout links, 120–122
Browse button, 99
bubble charts, 54–56
Build And View Analysis screen
ActionLinks, 105
column sorting, 36
contents, 27–29
embedded reports, 139
report navigation, 99
report views, 40
tables, 44–45
bulb gauges, 63
bulleted list tags, 19
bwith value in Go URLs, 96

B

<B> tags, 16, 18
Back To Application Customization
link, 117
background
charts, 51
column font color, 31
Gauge view, 62
bar charts, 55
Bar-Specific Properties window, 63
Before option for pivot tables,
74, 78, 80
bet value in Go URLs, 97
<BODY> tags, 17
bold tags, 16, 18
bookmark tags, 20
borders
charts, 51
columns, 31
gauges, 61–62
inline frames, 141

C

call value in Go URLs, 97
Campaign records
ActionLinks, 107
text format links, 110
cany value in Go URLs, 96
captions and Caption field
charts, 49
columns, 34
dashboard links, 119
Gauge view, 62
report navigation, 99
tags, 22
cells, columns, 31–32
Chart Component field, 53
Chart Position field, 80
Chart Title field, 64
Chart Type Special window, 54, 84
charts
area, 54–55
bubble, 55–56

funnel, 64–65
horizontal bar, 55
line, 56–57
line bar combo, 57
Pareto, 57–58
pie, 58
pivot, 80–84
radar, 59
report navigation from, 101–102
scatter, 59
step, 60
vertical bar, 56
views and settings, 45–54
Choose Request window for dashboard
  links, 119
Clear All Existing Filters Before Applying
  option, 39
color
  charts, 51, 53
  in columns, 31
  Gauge view, 61–62, 64
  pivot charts, 83–84
Color Selector, 31, 64
Column Format tab
  embedded reports, 146
  report navigation, 100
  settings, 32–34
Column Properties window, 30
  ActionLinks, 105–106
  Column Format tab, 32–34
  Conditional Format tab, 34–35
  Data Format tab, 34
  hyperlinks, 103–104
  report navigation, 99–100
  Style tab, 31–32
  text format links, 108
Column value in Go URLs, 98
columns and Column Properties
  window, 30
  ActionLinks, 105–106
  adding, removing, and
    reordering, 29

Column Format tab, 32–34
Conditional Format tab, 34–35
Data Format tab, 34
filters, 36–38
formatting, 29–30
funnel charts, 64
hyperlinks, 103–104
pivot tables, 66–69, 72–80
report navigation, 99–100
sorting, 36
Style tab, 31–32
tables, 42–43
text format links, 108
comments in HTML, 17
Company Profiles settings, 7–9
concatenating strings, 113
Conditional tab, 83
Conditional Format tab, 34–35
Contact records
  ActionLinks, 107
  text format links, 110
Content Properties window, 71–72
copying filters, 38
Create/Edit Filter window, 34–39, 83
Create Layout view, 143
cross-tab matrices, 66
csv value in Go URLs, 95
Current Window option, 120
Custom CSS Style Options (HTML
  Only) settings, 105–106
custom headings for columns, 33
Custom Object records, 111–112
custom report menus, 152–153
Custom Search tab, 153–154
custom text format, 108–112, 124–125
Custom Web Applet edit screen,
  147–148
Custom Web Tab screen, 149–150
Customization Customize Application
  privilege, 7

Customization: Layout Customize
  Application - Manage Dynamic
  Layouts privilege, 6
Customization: Layout Customize
  Application - Manage Homepage
  Customization privilege, 6
Customization: Layout Manage
  Homepage Custom Report
  privilege, 6

D

d value in Go URLs, 93
Dashboard Editor, 118, 122,
  133–134, 139
dashboard links, 12, 118
    breakout, 120–122
    embedded reports as, 122–123
    filtered, 124
    properties, 118–120
    tags, 123
Dashboard tab, 120–121, 133
dashboards
    Company Profile settings, 7–9
    Delete option, 140
    Display Results option, 135–136
    Modify Request option, 139
    Rename window, 139–140
    Report Links option, 136–138
    inside reports, 145–146
    reports inside, 133–135
    role-based access, 153
    Show View option, 138–139
    on web tabs, 149–152
Data Format tab
    ActionLinks, 106
    settings, 34, 103–104
    text format links, 108
Data Labels settings, 46
<DD> tags, 19
Default Analytics Look In setting, 9
default borders for inline frames, 141

Default Compound View
  selection, 138
definition tags, 19
definition list tags, 19
definition term tags, 19
deleting
    embedded reports, 140
    filters, 38
    views, 41
Description field for embedded
  reports, 131
designing reports, 26
    basics, 26–29
    charts. *See* charts
    columns. *See* columns and
      Column Properties window
    filters. *See* filters
    pivot tables. *See* pivot tables
    views, 40–44, 60–64
detail screens, linking reports to, 105
dial gauges, 64
Dial Specific Properties window, 63
directory locations in URLs, 87
Display Column & Table Headings
  field, 44
Display Name field, 116
Display Options field, 117
Display Results settings
    embedded reports, 122,
      135–136
    Title view, 42
Display Saved Name option, 41
Display Selector, 44
Display Text field, 117
Displays The Execute Report
  Immediately option, 6
<DL> tags, 19
Download link, 136–138
Download value in Go URLs, 94
drop-down lists for pivot tables, 79
    <DT> tags, 19
duplicating pivot table columns, 73

E

e-mail links, 12, 124–125
Edit Chart View screen, 45
Edit Filter option, 38
Edit Format window
    conditional formatting, 35
    headings, 33
    labels, 43
    pivot tables, 67–69, 72–75,
        78, 80
    tables, 42
    view alignment, 41
Edit Formula button, 29
Edit screens
    linking reports to, 105
    links to, 114–115
Edit View screen, 41
    funnel charts, 64
    Gauge view, 60
    pivot tables, 66, 80
    scatter charts, 59
    tables, 43
Edit View Chart screen, 101–102
Edit View: Table screen, 42–44
Edit Web Link window, 116–117
Embed CRM On Demand Content
    screen, 154–155
embedded reports, 128
    applets inside, 147–149
    custom report menus, 152–153
    Custom Search tab, 153–154
    dashboards inside, 145–146
    inside dashboards, 133–135
    Delete button, 140
    Display Results option, 135–136
    embedding process, 141–144
    external sites inside, 157–159
    on Home tab, 129–133
    iFrame tag for, 140–141
    as links, 122–123
    Modify Request option, 122, 139
    overview, 11–14
    Rename window, 139
    report widgets, 154–156
    Reports tab, 136–138
    role-based dashboard
        access, 153
    Show View option, 138–139
    on web tabs, 149–152
Enable Alternating Row "Green Bar"
    Styling option, 44
Enable Column Sorting In Dashboards
    option, 44
encoding in URLs, 89–90
end tags in HTML, 16
eq value in Go URLs, 95
ewith value in Go URLs, 96
excel value in Go URLs, 95
exclamation points (!) in tags, 17
Execute Report Immediately
    option, 131
Explode Wedge option, 58
external links, 125–126
external sites embedded inside reports,
    157–159

F

f value in Go URLs, 93
Factor Required To Meet Target
    field, 65
Favorite Lists Widget, 155
filter value in Go URLs, 98
filtered dashboards, linking to, 124
filters
    columns, 36–38
    embedded reports, 144
    in Go URLs, 95–98
    groups, 38
    predefined, 38–39
    report data, 36
    report navigation, 101
    variables, 39–40

Folder field
    embedded reports, 131
    pivot tables, 69
font tags, 18
fonts
    columns, 31
    Gauge view, 61
Force Standard Shape And Equal Stage
    Widths option, 65
Format Chart Data window
    line color, 57
    pivot charts, 83
    settings, 52–53
    wedges, 58
Format Headings option, 72
Format Labels option, 69
Format tags in Go URLs, 94–95
Format Values option, 69
Format View button, 41
formatting
    pivot table columns, 72–80
    pivot tables, 67–71
    report columns, 29–30
    tables, 42–44
formulas, 102–104, 113–114
forward slashes (/) in URLs, 87
Frame Height field, 149
Frame Info screen, 91–92
Frame Width field, 149
frames, inline
    embedded reports, 140–141
    tags, 21, 23
Full Visibility option, 9
funnel charts, 64–65

G

Gauge Canvas Properties window, 61
Gauge Layout settings, 61
Gauge Ranges window, 62
Gauge view, 60–64
ge value in Go URLs, 96

General Chart Properties window
    pie charts, 58
    pivot charts, 82
    settings, 45–46
Getting Started window, 26–28
global web applets, 147
Go paths in URLs, 88
Go URLs, 87
    embedded reports, 142
    tags, 92–98
Google Maps API, 157–159
Graph field for charts, 45
greater than character (>) in
    formulas, 103
Grid Lines tab, 50–51, 83
grids
    pivot charts, 83
    scatter charts, 59
    settings, 50–51
groups of filters, 38
gt value in Go URLs, 96

H

<H> tags, 18
<HEAD> tags, 17
headings
    columns, 33
    HTML tags, 18
    pivot tables, 72
height and Height field
    charts, 46–47
    columns, 32
    embedded reports, 130–131
    Gauge view, 62
    inline frames, 141
Hide Repeated Values option, 78
Hide This Column option, 146
hiding
    columns, 32, 74, 77,
        79, 146
    paging controls, 43

Historical Subject Areas settings, 7, 9
Home tab
    applets, 147
    embedding reports on, 129–133
Homepage Custom Report Detail
    screen, 130–131
Homepage Custom Report link, 130
Homepage Layout Wizard screen, 132
horizontal bar charts, 55
horizontal rule tags, 18
hosted applications, 2–3
hosts in URLs, 87–88
<HR> tags, 18
HTML
    in formulas, 102–104
    hyperlink type, 12
    image tags, 20–21
    inline frame tags, 21, 23
    link tags, 20
    list tags, 19
    requirements, 16
    structure tags, 17
    table tags, 21–22
    text tags, 17–19
<HTML> tags, 17
hyperlinks, 12
    external, 125–126
    in formulas, 102–104
    in narrative view, 104–105, 114

I

<I> tags, 18
icon library window, 149–150
iFrame tags, 21, 23, 140–141
image tags, 20–21
<IMG> tags, 20
Index Of option, 76–77
inline frames
    embedded reports, 140–141
    tags, 21, 23
Insert Page Break field, 70

Integration: Widgets Embed CRM On
    Demand Widgets privilege, 7
Integration: Widgets Manage Custom
    Web Applets privilege, 7
Interaction tab
    charts, 51–52
    Gauge view, 63
italic tags, 18

K

Key User Information settings, 9

L

labels
    charts, 46–48, 55–56
    Gauge view, 62
    pivot tables, 74
Layout field, 120
layouts
    dashboard links, 120
    embedded reports, 131–133
le value in Go URLs, 96
Lead records
    ActionLinks, 107
    text format links, 110
Left tab
    pivot charts, 82
    titles, 47
Legend Location field, 61
Legend tab, 51
legends
    charts, 51, 55–56
    Gauge view, 61
    pivot charts, 83
<LI> tags, 19
like value in Go URLs, 97
Limited Choices hyperlink, 37–38
line bar combo charts, 53–54, 57
line break tags, 18

line charts, 53, 56–57
line markers, 50
Link - In A Separate Window option,
    123, 136
Link - Within The Dashboard option,
    122, 136
Link or Image Object, 118
Link Or Image Properties window,
    118–120
link tags, 20
linking reports, 86
        ActionLinks, 105–107
        custom text format links, 108–112
        dashboard. *See* dashboard links to
            Detail screens, 105
        e-mail links, 124–125
        to Edit screens, 105, 114–115
        external links, 125–126
        Go URLs in, 92–98
        hyperlinks in formulas, 102–104,
            113–114
        hyperlinks in narrative view,
            104–105, 114
        navigation in, 99–102
        overview, 11–14
        URLs in, 86–92
        Web Link fields, 115–117
        web tabs, 126
list tags, 19
list item tags, 19
local networks in URLs, 87
logarithmic scales in charts, 49
Logo field for Title view, 41
lt value in Go URLs, 96

M

m value in Go URLs, 93
mailto URLs, 119
Manage Custom Reports privilege, 5
Manage Custom Web Applets
    privilege, 154

Manage Dashboards privilege, 5
Manage Dashboards screen, 133–134
Manage Personal Reports privilege, 5
Manager Visibility option, 7, 9
maps, Google, 157–159
Marker Type field, 64
Maximum Threshold field, 64
Maximum Value option for charts, 49
Measure field, 64
Measure Labels option, 55–56
Measures area in pivot tables, 65–66,
    75–77
Message Center Widget, 155
mht value in Go URLs, 94
Minimum Threshold field, 64
Minimum Value option for charts, 49
Modify Criteria link, 88
Modify Request option, 122, 139
multitenant software as a service
    environments, 2
My Custom Homepage Report link,
    130–131

N

Narrative field for Google maps,
    157–158
narrative view
        embedded reports, 143–144, 146
        hyperlinks in, 104–105, 114
Navigate value in Go URLs, 93
navigating reports, 99–102
navigation link type, 12
Negative Format field, 46
neq value in Go URLs, 96
New Calculated Item option, 79
New Filter button, 29, 36
New Homepage Report button, 130
New Window option for dashboard
    links, 120
nnull value in Go URLs, 97
null value in Go URLs, 97

O

OCTYPE tags, 112–113
<OL> tags, 19
Operator field for filters, 37
Opportunity records
    ActionLinks, 107
    text format links, 110
Opportunity reports, 142
Options tags
    in Go URLs, 93
    in URLs, 88
OR connectors for filters, 38
Order By button, 36
Override Default Data Format
    option, 34
        chart views, 46, 48
        hyperlinks in formulas, 103
Override Defaults option
    chart views, 50–51
    pivot charts, 83

P

<P> tags, 18, 95–98
padding columns, 31–32
Page Layout link, 117
Page tag, 123
Pages area for pivot tables, 66, 71,
    79–80
paging controls in tables, 42–43
paragraph tags, 18
Pareto charts, 53, 57–58
paths in URLs, 87–88, 93
pdf value in Go URLs, 94
Percent Of option, 76
Percent Of Column option, 76
Percent Of Layer option, 76
Percent Of Section option, 76
Percentage Of Column Parent
    option, 76

Percentage Of Row Parent option, 76
Personal Homepage screen, 154
pie charts, 53–54, 58
pipe symbol (|) for concatenating
    strings, 113
pivot charts, 80–84
pivot tables
    columns, 66–69, 72–80
    Content Properties window,
        71–72
    Measures area, 65–66, 75–77
    overview, 65–66
    Pages area, 71, 79–80
    Rows area, 65–67, 73–74
    Sections area, 69–70, 77–79
    totals, 67–71
    view properties, 66–67
Place Value In New Row option, 78
planning, 15
plus signs (+) in formulas, 103
Postfix field for Google maps, 157
prebuilt reports, 4
predefined filters, 38–39
Prefix field for Google maps, 157
Preview Analysis button, 28
Print value in Go URLs, 94
Printer Friendly link, 136–138
privileges, 4–7
Product records, 110
Prompt value in Go URLs, 93
Properties window for URLs, 90–91
protocols in URLs, 87–88

R

r value in Go URLs, 93
radar charts, 59
range markers, 50
Record Type Access settings, 7–8
record type-specific web applets, 147
Refresh link, 136–137

removing
    pivot table columns, 73
    report columns, 29
Rename window for embedded
    reports, 139
reordering columns, 29
repeating values for columns, 32
REPLACE function, 102–103, 113
REPLUSER session variable, 39
Report Links option, 122, 135
Report Links window, 136–138
report menus, 152–153
Report Object Properties menu, 135
Report paths in URLs, 88
Reporting Subject Areas settings, 7
reports overview
    Company Profile settings, 7–9
    designing. *See* designing reports
    embedded. *See* embedded reports
    linking. *See* linking reports
    for URLs, 91
    User Profile settings, 9–10
Reports Widget, 156
Right tab
    pivot charts, 82
    titles, 47
Role-Based Can Read All Records
    option, 7
role-based dashboard access, 153
Role Management Wizard, 8, 151
role privileges, 4–7
Rotate Labels option, 47
Rows area in pivot tables, 65–67, 73–74
Rows Per Page field, 44

S

Scale tab, 62
scales
    charts, 48–50, 83
    Gauge view, 62
scatter charts, 59

Scatter graphs, 45
scroll bars, 141
Section Properties window, 70
Sections area for pivot tables, 69–70,
    77–79
Select Dashboard field, 120
Select Navigation Target button, 34
Service Request records
    ActionLinks, 107
    text format links, 110
Service Request reports, 142
Show Blank Rows option, 70
Show Border option, 62
Show Data As option, 76
Show New HTML button, 156
Show View option, 122, 138–139
showAddress command, 159
Simple List Widget, 155
size and Size field
    charts, 46–47
    columns, 31–32
    embedded reports, 130–131
    funnel charts, 65
    Gauge view, 62–63
    inline frames, 141
    pivot charts, 82
    pivot table columns, 72
    scatter charts, 59
slashes (/) in URLs, 87
software as a service (SaaS)
    environments, 2
Sort button, 30
sorting
    pivot table columns, 73–74
    report columns, 36, 44
spaces in URLs, 87
Specify Manually option, 49
spider web charts, 59
Start New Page Dropdown option, 79
start tags in HTML, 16
Started Time field, 41
step charts, 60

strings, concatenating, 113
structure tags in HTML, 17
Style field, 45
Style tab
    ActionLinks, 105–106
    Column Properties window, 31–32
Subtitle field, 41
summation button in pivot tables, 68
Symbol Type field, 53

T

Tab Access & Order screen, 151
Table view, 42–44, 129
tables
    formatting, 42–44
    pivot. *See* pivot tables
    tags, 2, 21–22
tags, 16
    dashboard links, 123
    Go URL, 92–98
    image, 20–21
    inline frame, 21, 23
    link, 20
    list, 19
    structure, 17
    table, 21–22
    text, 17–19
    in URLs, 88–89
Target Value For Final Stage Only
    option, 65
targets
    dashboard links, 120
    funnel charts, 65
    report navigation, 34, 99–102
    web link fields, 117
Task record, 110
<TD> tags, 22
Team Visibility option, 7–9
text
    charts, 51
    dashboard links, 119

e-mail links, 124–125
format links, 108–112
HTML tags, 17–19
<TH> tags, 22
Tick Marks & Scale Type settings, 49
Title view, 41–42, 129
titles and Title field
    chart views, 45
    funnel charts, 64
    Gauge view, 61
    pivot charts, 82–83
    tags, 17
top-level domains in URLs, 87
top value in Go URLs, 97
totals in pivot tables, 67–71
<TR> tags, 22
Treat Numbers As field, 46
Treat Text As field, 125
txt value in Go URLs, 95
Type field
    charts, 45
    embedding reports, 148
    Gauge view, 63
    widgets, 156

U

<UL> tags, 19
unordered list tags, 19
URL Destination option, 119
URLs (Uniform Resource Locators)
    dashboard links, 119
    Go URL tags, 92–98
    overview, 86–92
Use Custom CSS Class field, 106
Use Custom CSS Style field, 106
Use Dashboard Object Name As Link
    Text option, 139
User Profile, 7, 9–10
User records
    ActionLinks, 107
    text format links, 110

user roles privileges, 4
User Security Information settings, 9

V

Value field for filters, 37
variables for filters, 39–40
vertical bar charts, 56
views, 40–41
    charts. *See* charts
    funnel charts, 64–65
    Gauge, 60–64
    pivot charts, 80–84
    pivot tables. *See* pivot tables
    title, 41–42

W

web addresses
    dashboard links, 119
    Go URL tags, 92–98
    overview, 86–92

Web Link fields, 11, 115–117
Web Link Target field, 117
web link type, 12
web tabs
    custom, 152
    embedded reports on, 149–152
    links to, 126
widgets, 154–156
width and Width field
    charts, 46–47
    columns, 32
    embedded reports, 130–131
    Gauge view, 62
    inline frames, 141
    pivot table columns, 72
wildcards in pivot tables, 74

X

xml value in Go URLs, 95

GET YOUR FREE SUBSCRIPTION TO *ORACLE MAGAZINE*

Oracle Magazine is essential gear for today's information technology professionals. Stay informed and increase your productivity with every issue of *Oracle Magazine*. Inside each free bimonthly issue you'll get:

- Up-to-date information on Oracle Database, Oracle Application Server, Web development, enterprise grid computing, database technology, and business trends
- Third-party news and announcements
- Technical articles on Oracle and partner products, technologies, and operating environments
- Development and administration tips
- Real-world customer stories

If there are other Oracle users at your location who would like to receive their own subscription to *Oracle Magazine*, please photo-copy this form and pass it along.

Three easy ways to subscribe:

① Web
Visit our Web site at **oracle.com/oraclemagazine**
You'll find a subscription form there, plus much more

② Fax
Complete the questionnaire on the back of this card
and fax the questionnaire side only to **+1.847.763.9638**

③ Mail
Complete the questionnaire on the back of this card
and mail it to **P.O. Box 1263, Skokie, IL 60076-8263**

ORACLE

Want your own FREE subscription?

To receive a free subscription to *Oracle Magazine*, you must fill out the entire card, sign it, and date it (incomplete cards cannot be processed or acknowledged). You can also fax your application to +1.847.763.9638. **Or subscribe at our Web site at oracle.com/oraclemagazine**

O **Yes, please send me a FREE subscription** *Oracle Magazine*.　　O No.

O From time to time, Oracle Publishing allows our partners exclusive access to our e-mail addresses for special promotions and announcements. To be included in this program, please check this circle. If you do not wish to be included, you will only receive notices about your subscription via e-mail.

O Oracle Publishing allows sharing of our postal mailing list with selected third parties. If you prefer your mailing address not to be included in this program, please check this circle.

If at any time you would like to be removed from either mailing list, please contact Customer Service at +1.847.763.9635 or send an e-mail to oracle@halldata.com. If you opt in to the sharing of information, Oracle may also provide you with e-mail related to Oracle products, services, and events. If you want to completely unsubscribe from any e-mail communication from Oracle, please send an e-mail to: unsubscribe@oracle-mail.com with the following in the subject line: REMOVE [your e-mail address]. For complete information on Oracle Publishing's privacy practices, please visit oracle.com/html/privacy.html

X _____　　　_____
signature (required)　　　　　　　　　　　date

name _____　　title _____

company _____　　e-mail address _____

street/p.o. box _____

city/state/zip or postal code _____　　telephone _____

country _____　　fax _____

Would you like to receive your free subscription in digital format instead of print if it becomes available? O Yes O No

YOU MUST ANSWER ALL 10 QUESTIONS BELOW.

① WHAT IS THE PRIMARY BUSINESS ACTIVITY OF YOUR FIRM AT THIS LOCATION? (check one only)

- ☐ 01 Aerospace and Defense Manufacturing
- ☐ 02 Application Service Provider
- ☐ 03 Automotive Manufacturing
- ☐ 04 Chemicals
- ☐ 05 Media and Entertainment
- ☐ 06 Construction/Engineering
- ☐ 07 Consumer Sector/Consumer Packaged Goods
- ☐ 08 Education
- ☐ 09 Financial Services/Insurance
- ☐ 10 Health Care
- ☐ 11 High Technology Manufacturing, OEM
- ☐ 12 Industrial Manufacturing
- ☐ 13 Independent Software Vendor
- ☐ 14 Life Sciences (biotech, pharmaceuticals)
- ☐ 15 Natural Resources
- ☐ 16 Oil and Gas
- ☐ 17 Professional Services
- ☐ 18 Public Sector (government)
- ☐ 19 Research
- ☐ 20 Retail/Wholesale/Distribution
- ☐ 21 Systems Integrator, VAR/VAD
- ☐ 22 Telecommunications
- ☐ 23 Travel and Transportation
- ☐ 24 Utilities (electric, gas, sanitation, water)
- ☐ 98 Other Business and Services ____

② WHICH OF THE FOLLOWING BEST DESCRIBES YOUR PRIMARY JOB FUNCTION? (check one only)

CORPORATE MANAGEMENT/STAFF
- ☐ 01 Executive Management (President, Chair, CEO, CFO, Owner, Partner, Principal)
- ☐ 02 Finance/Administrative Management (VP/Director/ Manager/Controller, Purchasing, Administration)
- ☐ 03 Sales/Marketing Management (VP/Director/Manager)
- ☐ 04 Computer Systems/Operations Management (CIO/VP/Director/Manager MIS/IS/IT, Ops)

IS/IT STAFF
- ☐ 05 Application Development/Programming Management
- ☐ 06 Application Development/Programming Staff
- ☐ 07 Consulting
- ☐ 08 DBA/Systems Administrator
- ☐ 09 Education/Training
- ☐ 10 Technical Support Director/Manager
- ☐ 11 Other Technical Management/Staff
- ☐ 98 Other

③ WHAT IS YOUR CURRENT PRIMARY OPERATING PLATFORM (check all that apply)

- ☐ 01 Digital Equipment Corp UNIX/VAX/VMS
- ☐ 02 HP UNIX
- ☐ 03 IBM AIX
- ☐ 04 IBM UNIX
- ☐ 05 Linux (Red Hat)
- ☐ 06 Linux (SUSE)
- ☐ 07 Linux (Oracle Enterprise)
- ☐ 08 Linux (other)
- ☐ 09 Macintosh
- ☐ 10 MVS
- ☐ 11 Netware
- ☐ 12 Network Computing
- ☐ 13 SCO UNIX
- ☐ 14 Sun Solaris/SunOS
- ☐ 15 Windows
- ☐ 16 Other UNIX
- ☐ 98 Other
- ☐ 99 None of the Above

④ DO YOU EVALUATE, SPECIFY, RECOMMEND, OR AUTHORIZE THE PURCHASE OF ANY OF THE FOLLOWING? (check all that apply)

- ☐ 01 Hardware
- ☐ 02 Business Applications (ERP, CRM, etc.)
- ☐ 03 Application Development Tools
- ☐ 04 Database Products
- ☐ 05 Internet or Intranet Products
- ☐ 06 Other Software
- ☐ 07 Middleware Products
- ☐ 99 None of the Above

⑤ IN YOUR JOB, DO YOU USE OR PLAN TO PURCHASE ANY OF THE FOLLOWING PRODUCTS? (check all that apply)

SOFTWARE
- ☐ 01 CAD/CAE/CAM
- ☐ 02 Collaboration Software
- ☐ 03 Communications
- ☐ 04 Database Management
- ☐ 05 File Management
- ☐ 06 Finance
- ☐ 07 Java
- ☐ 08 Multimedia Authoring
- ☐ 09 Networking
- ☐ 10 Programming
- ☐ 11 Project Management
- ☐ 12 Scientific and Engineering
- ☐ 13 Systems Management
- ☐ 14 Workflow

HARDWARE
- ☐ 15 Macintosh
- ☐ 16 Mainframe
- ☐ 17 Massively Parallel Processing
- ☐ 18 Minicomputer
- ☐ 19 Intel x86(32)
- ☐ 20 Intel x86(64)
- ☐ 21 Network Computer
- ☐ 22 Symmetric Multiprocessing
- ☐ 23 Workstation Services

SERVICES
- ☐ 24 Consulting
- ☐ 25 Education/Training
- ☐ 26 Maintenance
- ☐ 27 Online Database
- ☐ 28 Support
- ☐ 29 Technology-Based Training
- ☐ 30 Other
- ☐ 99 None of the Above

⑥ WHAT IS YOUR COMPANY'S SIZE? (check one only)

- ☐ 01 More than 25,000 Employees
- ☐ 02 10,001 to 25,000 Employees
- ☐ 03 5,001 to 10,000 Employees
- ☐ 04 1,001 to 5,000 Employees
- ☐ 05 101 to 1,000 Employees
- ☐ 06 Fewer than 100 Employees

⑦ DURING THE NEXT 12 MONTHS, HOW MUCH DO YOU ANTICIPATE YOUR ORGANIZATION WILL SPEND ON COMPUTER HARDWARE, SOFTWARE, PERIPHERALS, AND SERVICES FOR YOUR LOCATION? (check one only)

- ☐ 01 Less than $10,000
- ☐ 02 $10,000 to $49,999
- ☐ 03 $50,000 to $99,999
- ☐ 04 $100,000 to $499,999
- ☐ 05 $500,000 to $999,999
- ☐ 06 $1,000,000 and Over

⑧ WHAT IS YOUR COMPANY'S YEARLY SALES REVENUE? (check one only)

- ☐ 01 $500, 000, 000 and above
- ☐ 02 $100, 000, 000 to $500, 000, 000
- ☐ 03 $50, 000, 000 to $100, 000, 000
- ☐ 04 $5, 000, 000 to $50, 000, 000
- ☐ 05 $1, 000, 000 to $5, 000, 000

⑨ WHAT LANGUAGES AND FRAMEWORKS DO YOU USE? (check all that apply)

- ☐ 01 Ajax
- ☐ 02 C
- ☐ 03 C++
- ☐ 04 C#
- ☐ 05 Hibernate
- ☐ 06 J++/J#
- ☐ 07 Java
- ☐ 08 JSP
- ☐ 09 .NET
- ☐ 10 Perl
- ☐ 11 PHP
- ☐ 12 PL/SQL
- ☐ 13 Python
- ☐ 14 Ruby/Rails
- ☐ 15 Spring
- ☐ 16 Struts
- ☐ 17 SQL
- ☐ 18 Visual Basic
- ☐ 98 Other

⑩ WHAT ORACLE PRODUCTS ARE IN USE AT YOUR SITE? (check all that apply)

ORACLE DATABASE
- ☐ 01 Oracle Database 11*g*
- ☐ 02 Oracle Database 10*g*
- ☐ 03 Oracle9*i* Database
- ☐ 04 Oracle Embedded Database (Oracle Lite, Times Ten, Berkeley DB)
- ☐ 05 Other Oracle Database Release

ORACLE FUSION MIDDLEWARE
- ☐ 06 Oracle Application Server
- ☐ 07 Oracle Portal
- ☐ 08 Oracle Enterprise Manager
- ☐ 09 Oracle BPEL Process Manager
- ☐ 10 Oracle Identity Management
- ☐ 11 Oracle SOA Suite
- ☐ 12 Oracle Data Hubs

ORACLE DEVELOPMENT TOOLS
- ☐ 13 Oracle JDeveloper
- ☐ 14 Oracle Forms
- ☐ 15 Oracle Reports
- ☐ 16 Oracle Designer
- ☐ 17 Oracle Discoverer
- ☐ 18 Oracle BI Beans
- ☐ 19 Oracle Warehouse Builder
- ☐ 20 Oracle WebCenter
- ☐ 21 Oracle Application Express

ORACLE APPLICATIONS
- ☐ 22 Oracle E-Business Suite
- ☐ 23 PeopleSoft Enterprise
- ☐ 24 JD Edwards EnterpriseOne
- ☐ 25 JD Edwards World
- ☐ 26 Oracle Fusion
- ☐ 27 Hyperion
- ☐ 28 Siebel CRM

ORACLE SERVICES
- ☐ 28 Oracle E-Business Suite On Demand
- ☐ 29 Oracle Technology On Demand
- ☐ 30 Siebel CRM On Demand
- ☐ 31 Oracle Consulting
- ☐ 32 Oracle Education
- ☐ 33 Oracle Support
- ☐ 98 Other
- ☐ 99 None of the Above